The Freedom Within

Gerry Hussey is a performance psychologist who has been working in the fields of health and performance for almost twenty years.

Through his programmes, keynote speaking engagements and events, Gerry helps clients strip away learned behaviours and thinking patterns to unclutter, clarify and overcome both internal and external obstacles and challenges, and ignite the best version of themselves from a mind, body and spirit perspective.

At the forefront of building high-performance teams and individuals, Gerry leads teams for success at high-profile competitions such as the Olympic Games, Heineken Cups, World Cups, and World and European championships. He also works with corporate organisations along with one-on-one sessions for individuals.

Gerry brings an unrivalled wealth of honesty, experience and infectious passion to everything he does. He has the ability to awaken, unlock and connect people and teams in a truly powerful manner.

Find Gerry at www.soulspace.ie or on Instagram @gerry_hussey or @soulspace_the_experience

THE
FREEDOM
WITHIN

Gerry Hussey

HACHETTE
BOOKS
IRELAND

First published in Ireland in 2023 by HACHETTE BOOKS IRELAND

1

The image of the brain used in the text is reproduced
with permission from Designua/shutterstock.com.

Cataloguing in Publication Data is available from the British Library.

ISBN 9781399727082

Typeset in ArnoPro by Bookends Publishing Services, Dublin
Printed and bound in Great Britain byClays Ltd, Elcograf S.p.A.

Some names and identifying details have been changed within
this book. Any resulting resemblance to persons, living or dead,
is entirely coincidental and unintentional.

This publication is not intended as a substitute for
the advice of healthcare professionals.

Hachette Books Ireland policy is to use papers that are natural, renewable
and recyclable products and made from wood grown in sustainable forests.
The logging and manufacturing processes are expected to conform to
the environmental regulations of the country of origin.

Hachette Books Ireland
8 Castlecourt Centre
Castleknock
Dublin 15, Ireland

A division of Hachette UK Ltd
Carmelite House, 50 Victoria Embankment, London EC4Y 0DZ

www.hachettebooksireland.ie

To my incredible wife, you are my rock and my light.
Thank you for loving me when I couldn't love myself.
Thank you for your unrelenting love, compassion and
gentle but powerful strength that holds me together at my
weakest moments. You ignite my soul, and you are the
loving force that gels our family together.
Without you I am lost; with you I am at home.
This book and everything you allow me to do and be is for you.

Author's Note

If you picked up this book, chances are you are a little curious and maybe a little stuck in where you are in your life.

You might find yourself dwelling in unhelpful emotions like fear, overwhelm, anger and guilt while endlessly chasing something intangible to help you feel more successful or 'enough', losing sight of the incredible gifts you already have.

Maybe you are simply tired of chasing.

What if the life you dream of is possible and that a life of greater inner ease and joy is available to you?

What if the emotions you felt when you woke in the morning were love and gratitude, and as you fell asleep were connection, trust and peace?

Would you want it? Would you be willing to work for it? Would you be willing to open your mind and your heart to this book?

It's time to dare to believe again, to dream again, to let go, to come home to your deepest gift, to discover emotional freedom and your superpower: emotional choice.

In the following pages, I endeavour to share with you simple but powerful examples and methods that will lead you to a whole new level of emotional awareness, emotional regulation and good emotional health. We touched upon some of the topics in my first book, *Awaken Your Power Within*, but here in *The Freedom Within* we go deeper.

In this book, I challenged myself to focus on one big topic – emotional health – and in doing so I delved deeper than I ever have before into certain other topics such as beliefs, family dynamics, conscious awareness, emotional states, emotional freedom and what good emotional health means.

As ever, my wish is that in sharing my story and my experiences I will help others come to know and understand themselves better. I really hope that you enjoy this journey with me.

Contents

Introduction

My greatest awakening

The sound of silence is deafening; my heart feels like it's being physically pulled out of my chest through my ribcage. I am struggling to breathe, my mind racing with a million self-destructive thoughts, and I can feel myself drowning in an ocean of fear, regret and sadness, all of course disguised as anger.

Upstairs I can hear my wife, Miriam, putting my son, Eli, to bed. I can hear them laughing and singing, but in Miriam's voice, in her energy, I can hear she is pulled between putting her son to bed and getting downstairs to stop her husband from drowning. Right now it feels like I am in a different universe to them. I hear Eli's happiness and know that he is oblivious to the struggle going on inside his dad. I hope he always knows happiness and joy and that he never has to deal with the intensity of the emotions I am experiencing right now. The inner critic that I have worked so hard to understand

and silence has somehow returned with more spite and venom than ever before and he is attacking me for the situation I am in now – but, seemingly, as payback for years of keeping him silent.

The dinner I have just cooked sits on the island, cold. My stomach is in such a knot that not only can I not imagine eating it, I can't imagine ever eating again. I push it to one side and as I do I notice my hand is shaking, shivering in fear.

There is a heaviness in my heart, a feeling of dread, of being pulled into the abyss of failure and loneliness. All I can hear is my dad's voice as he struggled to get the words out, struggled to know what to say or to understand what I had done. I hear the surprise and the hurt in his voice and, of course, I blame myself for all of it.

'Have you spoken to your mother about it?' he had said earlier on the phone, referring to the publication of my new book *Awaken Your Power Within*, 'she was looking for you.' I know what he is really saying: Have you any idea how upset she is? And I know he wants to ask me how I could do this to her. Because in my book, I had written about the anxiety and depression I had experienced as a child. I knew my mother would be worried about me, and in my heart I was afraid that in some way my speaking about this would make her feel that she had done a bad job when in fact, as people who read my first book will know, without my mother's steadfast love, I simply would not be here today. Knowing how special and important she is to me made me even more afraid that I might have hurt her.

The inner critical Gerry is very good at going to worst-case scenario and he is doing it better than ever now. The inner critic that I had worked so hard to heal had found something painful to cling to. As we will discover later in this book, very often the place of our greatest emotional pain is the place where we still need to heal and I was quickly discovering I had some important healing to do, but at that moment I didn't have that perspective. I simply had a voice in my head saying, 'Why did you do this? Why are you hurting people? Is your truth really that important? Do you really have to tell your story? You are selfish and you are a bad person.' And in that moment I was submerged in a tidal wave of fear, shame and guilt.

I realise that Miriam is standing at the door. There is a moment of silence where, as only Miriam can do, she is totally there in that space, with me and for me. She understands how I feel and at the same time there is a courage and a strength in her that reminds me that I knew this was never going to be easy. That maybe this is the final part of me becoming free. As we will explore later in the book, emotional freedom, as a fundamental part of emotional health, isn't always easy. Staying trapped is easy. With all growth comes pain. I was on the cusp of a whole new life of freedom but I first had to pass through incredible emotional pain. So much of me longed to shut down and to run away from my emotions and yet there was a piece of me that knew that beyond this place of emotional pain is emotional freedom.

Miriam holds me for a second and, in that second, I stop

falling. Then she smiles and looks me in the eye. 'You are amazing and you are going to help so many people and I love you.' She then pushes me back a little, reminding me that there is somewhere I need to be. 'You go on in, the laptop is set up, take a minute and I will bring you a cup of tea.' I look at the clock: it's 8.30 p.m. and time to click the link.

What is this terrible thing that I have done that has spun me into such a negative place? I have written a book – a book about my life, my darkest days during my childhood, and my deepest struggles: something I put my heart and soul, and twenty years of my greatest lessons, into. My wish was that others would find in it inspiration, hope and meaning, and a way not to feel alone like I did for years. I had truly believed that that book, *Awaken Your Power Within*, would be my final step into freedom. Little did I know that after 20 years and many forward steps on the road to mental and emotional freedom, this current book, *The Freedom Within*, would be the hardest to write and that the process of doing so would test everything I thought I knew and believed about myself.

As I walk out of my kitchen to click the link to welcome thousands of people online to celebrate the publication of *Awaken Your Power Within*, I take a second to stop and breathe and I hear myself saying to Miriam, 'I wish I'd never written the damn thing.'

Awakening your power is the first powerful step, but emotional health and learning to really believe in and love yourself is where the deepest freedom begins. I thought that I had done the work. I truly believed that I was happy with the person I was and was content in my life and all that I had achieved. What I discovered on the publication of *Awaken Your Power Within* was that my happiness was still dependent on what other people thought of me, on other people's actions, words and feelings.

I had learned to distance myself from all of that. Those people didn't know who I was deep down, so their opinions didn't impact how I felt about myself. I thought that this was freedom. But when the book came out, I discovered that I still cared deeply and was attached to what my family – those who knew me the best – thought about me and my work. I still sought external validation and approval. I was terrified that writing what I did in *Awaken Your Power Within* would make my family stop loving me. I still needed their acceptance and approval. Would they still love me? Would they still allow me to be part of their world? Could I still play the same old role in the same old way? I could not risk the familiar. I was trapped with an absolute need for my family's approval. All the emotional wounds I had been carrying my entire life came to the surface. Emotionally, I was still a scared, lost eight-year-old boy.

After years of thinking about, dreaming about, crafting, shaping and eventually writing my first book and the pride and joy I had in it, I became crippled with an overwhelming sense of fear and disappointment. And I thought what if I could never escape this feeling? Would I always need to prove my worth to other people? Why wasn't I emotionally free enough to realise that I was enough? Was this the way it was always going to be: a lifetime of incredible experiences but with that constant undercurrent of fear about what other people think? There had to be a different way.

On the book's release in 2021, I discovered that the next step in my journey needed to go deeper. Over the years I had been pursuing a life that was important to me and the things that made me happy and filled my heart with love. Slowly and quietly I had built my life from a place of love, creating and nurturing a business that I was passionate about, purchasing a home I dreamed of and doing it quietly without fuss. But now I was beginning to realise that I was doing it quietly for a reason. I still didn't fully, truly and deeply believe in myself. I still didn't want to annoy people. I was afraid to be seen in a certain way. I didn't want to step on anyone's toes. I was still emotionally imprisoned in my past.

I needed to begin living my life on my terms and the only way to do that was to really examine my emotional health – the unconscious emotional wounds I was carrying, the beliefs and values that were no longer serving me. I had written a book, the book was selling out quicker than we could get it onto the shelves, I was on radio and TV and in newspapers and I had now lost the ability to do things quietly. It was time to have the courage to speak my truth with passion and belief and to back myself 100 per cent. It was time to embrace the new life I had worked so hard to create.

As the publicity and the buzz from my first book died

down, I began to see that I had now reached another layer of change and evolution – another challenge. I knew that I had two choices: run from the discomfort, ignore it, mask it, hide it; or else stop, breathe, listen, acknowledge and then act. It was time for me to take the next step.

In the days and weeks that followed, a question became clear in my mind: how can I begin living an emotionally healthy and ultimately free life?

If we think of a garden, weeds can grow easily; with little or no attention they can grow wherever they want. But to have a beautiful garden of flowers, flowers that you love and that you have chosen, you have to be deliberate in how you prepare, what you plant and how you manage the garden and the soil, the seeds and the environment. Our emotional garden can very easily become filled with weeds if we don't attend to it in the right way – if we don't plant the right seeds, nurture the new plants and prune back where necessary. To have an emotional garden that blossoms with the right things we must be willing to do the work.

It is my hope that this book will be a practical guide to empower you to look deeply at the emotions that are currently driving you and to ask yourself are those emotions healing or hurting you, enabling or disabling you.

Facing the unknown

We know that in life, we can't always control what happens to us. We can't control what other people say or think about us and we can't control other people's actions. As long as our emotions, our happiness and our success is dependent on the external world, then we will always live in a world where we have an inner sense of uncertainty, unpredictability, overwhelm and fear. The ability to regulate our inner emotions is one of the most important skills to have if we want to regulate and navigate our external world with greater ease and conscious awareness.

In this book we will examine how we, as humans, have an incredible freedom – the freedom to choose how we respond. We can begin to release ourselves from our unmet emotional needs and the struggles of trying to resist, predict or control what is happening outside of us. Emotionally healthy people will at times feel anger, judgement, sadness. But they have the ability to recognise that they are in a destructive emotional state and they have the freedom and the power to choose to move out of this state. Emotional health does not protect us from at times feeling all types of human emotions. In fact, as humans, we're meant to feel every human emotion.

The analogy I use is that we can be thermometers or thermostats. A thermometer is a very important thing: it tells us what the current state of the environment is – but it does nothing to change the environment. Some people are like thermometers, constantly describing, constantly telling us what the environment is. Constantly identifying the problems with the environment – but crucially, not doing anything to change it. On the other hand, a thermostat can take a cold environment and make it warm, or make a warm environment cooler. Some people are like that: not only can they identify and recognise what the outside condition is, but they can work to change it into what they want it to be. As human beings we have to ask ourselves are we thermostats or thermometers? Are we here simply to describe the outer environment or are we here to change it into what we want it to be?

We have the ability to release ourselves from a victim mentality and from a belief that life is happening to us; instead we can begin to ask why something is happening for us, what we are here to learn.

Emotional freedom is emotional health

We spend so much of our lives searching and striving for things we think will make us happy. But very often, when we eventually get these things we realise that either they don't make us happy or there is still something missing, and the inner search for something else continues.

I believe, however, that there is something even beyond happiness that is more powerful and more desirable. And that is emotional freedom. Happiness, like all emotions, can be temporary, and in the ever-changing fortunes of life it is not possible or even appropriate to be happy all the time. In fact, at certain times it is healthy to experience other emotions and if we see happiness as the only desirable or good emotion, we may very well see or judge all other emotions as wrong or undesirable.

In order to have true peace, we need freedom from our ego and all its self-created identifications, beliefs and limitations. Freedom from other people's ideas and beliefs about us, freedom from the emotional highs of flattery and the emotional lows of criticism, and from the unhealthy roles we get caught up in playing over and over in all of our relationships – even our closest ones.

True peace often requires us to let go of any predetermined ideas of who we need to be or indeed how the world should be. Instead we need to allow the world to be as it is while maintaining clarity and certainty about who we need to be. Emotional health requires freedom from the fear of failure, from the thought that we will arrive at the end of our life with regrets that we have never actually lived.

A country can't be at peace until it has autonomy and freedom; as human beings we can't have peace until we have emotional freedom.

In this book, I will look at how we can break free from the harmful emotions that are holding us back – fear, anger, disappointment, shame and guilt – and how we can realign our beliefs and values to live lives of inner peace and true authenticity. Our emotional choice, on any given day, in any given situation, is one of the most powerful choices we will make because the emotions we feel and the emotions we maintain play such an important role in every aspect of our lives, from our happiness to our sense of freedom, our ability to manifest the life we dream of, right down to our physical health and well-being.

The past three years have been a journey of internal work, examining the deepest parts of myself – parts I thought that I had already healed.

I have gone on a powerful journey of self-examination and deep awakening. I had to learn how to love and accept myself on a level deeper than anything I had ever imagined. In doing so, I let go of the unhealthy emotional need for approval and I recognised that, as important as other people in my life are, I cannot live my life for them or for their approval: I have to give myself the freedom to live it for myself.

I now faced a really important question: is it possible for me to live a life of total freedom, freedom to be who I choose to be, freedom to speak my truth, freedom to manifest the life I dream, freedom to simply be free to enjoy life? The answer of course is yes. It is possible, not just for me but for all of us. Opening up to ourselves, really allowing ourselves to trust in our own inherent goodness and worthiness, is the first step to living a life of true emotional health.

Many people have been asking what has taken me so long to write this second book. The answer is I don't want to simply write books. I want to capture in the most human and honest way the biggest awakenings and lessons of my life, and it takes time to work through these and see what really works and what is just theory. Developing the techniques and then writing this book has been a powerful journey for me. I have liberated myself in a way I never believed was possible, one that has allowed me to be present in my own life, where I am no longer a passive passenger in my emotions or in my life; instead I am an active and conscious creator that has become free to live and love, and on my own terms.

This book is a life journey of breaking free from self-imprisoning emotions of fear and transforming an entire external world by transforming an inner emotional state. I hope it can be the beginning of the awakening of your greatest gift, the gift of emotional freedom.

The book is divided into a number of different sections. Each will take us on a powerful deep dive into the reality of our emotional world, and as we progress we will ask and answer the most powerful and liberating questions that will enable us to arrive at a whole new level of emotional awareness and emotional freedom.

The Truth About Emotions

Time to think about our emotional health

Emotions, as we know, can be uplifting, joyous, life-giving, or they can be debilitating and life-disabling. They can hold us in the past, through shame and guilt, they can propel us into the future with passion and enthusiasm and they can centre us in the present moment with joy and gratitude. Over recent years there has been so much focus on mental health and understanding our thoughts and now I believe the future of health also requires us to look more deeply at emotional health, what good emotional health is and how we can all experience far greater levels of it.

So what is good emotional health?

Good emotional health ensures that we have the ability to refocus ourselves, to live within a state of inner calm and with resilience, empathy and awareness of our own needs and the needs of others. It's like our inner compass; our inner wisdom knows that the ultimate state we should be achieving is one of peace and calm. When we begin to know ourselves more, to understand where our emotions come from and the reason we react in an emotional way to certain situations and triggers, we are on the path to good emotional health and to living a life that is more committed to peace than anger, to love than fear, to non-judgement than judgement. When we are committed to inner peace, we can choose to let everything else go; when we are committed more to our own happiness than our own suffering and when we are committed to making this world a better place, we fill ourselves with positive and healing love. Our emotions fluctuate less and we begin to live with this inner freedom, this inner emotional bliss.

When we are in emotional dis-health, however, we can operate from a place of fear, worry, anxiety and stress, where we catastrophise about what is happening in our lives and the future. We find ourselves stuck in negative thought patterns that can be difficult to break free from.

Operating from a place of strong or good emotional health is fundamental to our long-term health and happiness. By obtaining optimum emotional health, we are able to navigate and recover from the challenges life throws at us. Our stresses and worries are put into perspective and we can begin living according to our true purpose. When we operate from a place of good emotional health we begin to develop a heightened awareness where we realise that the way we focus on something, the words we use, the narrative we use to describe the situation, either magnifies the problem or magnifies the solution. We are either magnifying our own problems or we are magnifying our own freedom.

When we begin to let resistance, anger and judgement go, when we take away our attention from the things we can't control and focus only on the things we can control, when we move from emotional reactions to emotional responses, we become emotionally free. By 'free', I don't mean that sometimes we won't suffer negative emotions. Emotionally healthy people will at times suffer anger, judgement, sadness. But they are empowered to move out of these emotions with more ease and, ultimately, begin living with an inner state of peace, calmness and love.

> 'When we begin to let resistance and anger and judgement go, when we take away our attention from the things we can't control and focus only on the things we can control, when we move from emotional reactions to emotional responses, we become emotionally free.'

I will use the terms 'emotional regulation' and 'emotional disregulation' throughout the book. Emotional regulation describes our ability to effectively manage and respond to an emotional experience in a healthy and timely manner, to exert control over our own emotional state.

Emotional disregulation, on the other hand, refers to the inability of a person to control or regulate their emotional response. There are many factors that can cause emotional disregulation in a person. Early psychological traumas due to abuse or neglect from parents or significant caregivers in the key developmental years are among the most important and we will discuss these in detail as we explore the issue of unmet emotional needs.

Press Pause

Recognising the difference between good emotional health and emotional dis-health

Imagine the following scenario: it's a beautiful sunny day and you're driving to work for an important meeting. Just a few miles from home, you discover that you have a puncture and have to pull over to the side of the road. Now you're stranded and have no way of getting to work. Your meeting starts in half an hour.

A person in emotional dis-health might throw their hands up in the air and write the entire day off as a bad case, fixating on their bad luck at getting a puncture at that moment, just when they needed to be in work. They might worry that if they don't show up for this meeting, it will look bad and their position at work might be called into question. The world seems to be set against them and they become the victim.

However, if that person had relatively good emotional health, they might view themselves as lucky that the puncture happened so close to home. That they were able to pull into a secure and safe housing estate and leave the car there while they went home and attended the meeting remotely. An emotionally healthy person would accept the puncture as an inconvenience but not allow it to dictate or ruin their entire day.

Which response would you have? Can you ask yourself 'Why is this happening for me?' as opposed to 'Why is this happening to me?'

Emotional bias

Focusing on what's wrong within ourselves and in the universe is always the easy thing to do, and emotionally responding to what's wrong or where the threat is is the easy state to be in. However, placing our energy and attention on what's right in ourselves and in the universe is also always available and a far more powerful way to live, but can be more difficult. This is because our brains and nervous systems are set up to do one job above all else – keep us alive – and the way they do that is by constantly scanning the world for threats and alerting us to them. We have a natural bias towards the detection of threat which means that if unchecked we can spend our lives living in an emotion of fear. Very often the emotions that speak the loudest are the ones that are fear based. Emotions such as fear, hate, anger, judgement and impatience are lower-energy emotions, so they require less effort and less energy to reach, but they're deeply destructive. The higher-energy, higher-vibrational emotions such as joy and gratitude are always available, but they're harder to attain, and they take work and practice.

HOW IS YOUR EMOTIONAL HEALTH?

Answer yes or no to the following questions. Really think about the answers and see if they surprise you or tell you anything about your emotional health.

1. Do you find it difficult to be present in the moment without thought of the future or the past?

---

2. When something unexpected happens, do you have the capacity to respond to it with calmness, perspective and confidence?
3. Do you find that you get over-emotional about situations that shouldn't really demand a high level of emotion?
4. Do you find it difficult to handle stressful situations?
5. Do you find that you fly off the handle easily and find it difficult to regulate your responses?
6. Do you find it hard to get emotionally excited about things that require emotional energy, or do you feel emotionally tired or drained?
7. Do you find simple everyday decisions overwhelming?
8. Do you find yourself catastrophising about the future?
9. When you wake up in the morning, do you feel a sense of calm and ease about the day ahead?
10. Do you regularly stop to savour your accomplishments and blessings?
11. Do you begin most days with the right emotional energy – calm, confident, assured, aligned, grounded, feeling safe, feeling secure?
12. Do you experience regular feelings of security and emotional safety?

Emotions are neither positive nor negative

Emotions are not the enemy and emotions are neither positive nor negative: they are simply information that gives us incredible and valuable insights. Emotions only have a negative consequence when they are blocked, suppressed or acted on in the wrong way. It is our reaction to our emotions that is the important thing; our reaction is what has a positive or negative impact on our lives. Once we learn to read emotions without judgement, we will realise that all emotions are simply important messengers.

Where we project our emotional reaction is rarely the cause of the emotion

When we reflect deeply on how we react to certain situations and events, we realise that the issue or person onto which we project our emotion is rarely actually the real issue. All emotions are simply information – information that points to something that needs to be addressed on a deeper level. Our emotional reaction is a message to ourselves about where we are attaching our attention and focus and whether that is a place of love or a place of fear, a place of pain or a place of power. For example, if you are in a work meeting and someone asks for a report that you are due to submit, your immediate emotional reaction might be shame that you haven't yet submitted the report. You become overly defensive and aggressive with the person who asked the question. But that simple question triggered an immediate emotional reaction from you because your unconscious emotional state is one of fear: that you're not good enough, that you need to earn your place in the world, that you have to prove your worth. When someone hurts us in a relationship, our emotional reaction might be anger, leading to feelings of resentment and hurt. But this emotion of anger, again, comes from a place of fear – fear of abandonment, that we are not enough.

All emotions are powerful messages that have far more to do with our inner world – our unconscious emotional state and our beliefs, inner stories and values – and less to do with the people and things in our outer world. The person, thing or situation in the outside world is simply the thing that has triggered our emotion or the target on which we are projecting our emotion. The more I live and observe, the more I am certain that the person, thing or situation that we project our emotions towards is rarely the root cause of those emotions. We can only express an emotion that we are holding. We can only express an emotion that we have generated, and the only person who can generate or hold an emotion in me is me. The root cause of the emotion is often something to do with our past, our deepest beliefs, our thinking habits, our expectations or our interpretation of what's happening in the outside world. That which has triggered the emotion is our teacher. Very often the place of our greatest emotional pain is the place of our greatest discovery.

Suppressing emotions depletes us of energy and vitality

Suppressing or denying an emotion is like pushing an air-filled ball underneath the water in a swimming pool. You may hold it down as long as you like, and as long as you maintain a conscious intent to hold it down and put active pressure on it, it will stay beneath the water. However, as soon as you let it go, as soon as you release the active pressure, it will pop back to the surface. Emotions are the same; if we simply suppress them or deny them or try to drown them out with distractions, we are not dealing with them and they are not going to go away. They will simply wait, and the moment we stop being distracted or the moment we stop suppressing them they will come to the top.

'For as long as we are suppressing an emotion our vital energy reserves are being depleted.'

We must also realise that, just like holding the ball under the water, suppressing an emotion requires active energy and conscious or unconscious attention. This means that for as long as we are suppressing an emotion our vital energy reserves are being depleted, and with suppressed emotions come suppressed immune systems.

Holding or suppressing emotions can cause fatigue, chronic stress and illness. I have often had clients come to me with consistent and overwhelming tiredness despite getting enough sleep, eating the right food and taking regular exercise. The amount of energy that is required to suppress an emotion is so great that our body has to prioritise its available energy for this task and so it starves our brain and our nervous system of the energy they require to function with vitality.

Fatigue and tiredness can of course be caused by the presence of something – for example, a challenge or a new baby or a project that requires all our attention. But we must be aware that fatigue and tiredness can also be caused by the lack of something. If we are suppressing emotions such as fear, frustration, jealousy and so on, then we are depleting vital energy reserves in doing so, and because these are the emotions that we are really feeling, there is little or no space for the emotions of love, joy, gratitude, adventure.

Meeting our emotional pain

Anybody who knows my story and my journey will know that I have been blessed to have a number of very special people coach, guide and mentor me over the years. One of the most important people in my life is a man called Ravi. Ravi has been an immense support, guide and friend to me over many years and is one of the greatest minds I have ever encountered. With gentle and humble questioning, he can quickly unpack a problem, challenge an inner narrative or subconscious belief and take me to a place of total clarity and a new level of self-awareness.

Ravi has an incredible understanding of human awareness and consciousness and ability to explain the human ego – how it shows up, why it shows up the way it does, and how we can begin to control it so that it serves us, ensuring we are no longer at its mercy. Ravi has taught me the true meaning of non-attachment, non-judgement and non-comparison, the foundational pillars of our journey to true emotional health and freedom which I explore later in the section 'The Freedom: A New Way of Living'. Ravi uses various methods to help people release emotion, release trauma and gain higher self awareness, such as massage, meditation and powerful conversations that inevitably lead his clients to a deeper knowledge of themselves. He creates an incredibly real, safe and open space where, before you know it, you are sharing your deepest truths and fears. Before I met Ravi I had heard so much about how powerful he was and that grown men could cry while receiving a massage from Ravi.

Of course, I had heard about him for years before I eventually found the courage to go and see him. My ego made every excuse for me not to go: I was too busy; I didn't have time; his practice was in the wrong part of the city; traffic was too heavy; I didn't really need a massage from Ravi – I was already on the path to self-awareness and was aware of the emotions bubbling beneath the surface. I had already done the work, or so I thought.

My brain went through all the usual nonsense that my ego came up with to try to convince me to stay in the familiar and the safe and to avoid pressing further on my own emotional wounds. I will explore the ego in more detail in the following section, 'The Awareness Shift' but this is the part of us that is always desperately clinging to the familiar and the safe, desperately asking us to hold on to our traumas, our hurts, our unconscious programmes, because it is terrified that if we were to change, if we were to finally let go of everything we think defines us, it would lose control over who we are.

After many years listening to my ego, however, I decided it was time to go to Ravi just to prove that I really didn't need him in my life and to prove to everybody that I was open to him but that he wasn't going to be able to tell me anything I didn't already know. Before I even met him I had convinced myself that I was going to show Ravi how open-minded and how free I was. I remember walking into his clinic that day already telling myself that this was a waste of time and that the quicker I got in and out the better.

Then, when I met Ravi, I was stopped in my tracks. There was something about him – a gentleness and a knowingness – that I will never forget. It was like he had been waiting for me all that time. But he couldn't have; he'd never met me before. Yet even before I opened my mouth, let alone my mind or my heart, I knew that he could see something in me that I couldn't see myself. He was looking at me in a way that simply said, *I know you, and you are welcome.*

I remember lying on his massage table, and as he moved his hands through the different parts of my neck and shoulders and back, the physical pain was excruciating. It was like he was touching raw nerves. As I squirmed, I became determined not to buckle under the pain. I gripped the table, my hands desperately holding on to the sides. In my mind I was telling myself, *He will not break me, I can endure this, I'm stronger than this, stand up to this pain, get through this.* In that first 15 minutes I hardly took a breath, sucking in, biting down, grasping the side of the table. I could feel the sweat beginning to roll down my forehead. I remember grabbing a wire underneath the table to try and withstand the pain.

As I lay there in agony, in total silence, my jaw and teeth clenched, getting through the pain, eventually Ravi stopped. He waited a few moments and then he knelt down beside me and said something that would become life-changing for me. 'For the past 15 minutes,' he said, 'you have been in pain, but you haven't expressed it, you haven't released it, you haven't screamed, and you haven't asked for help. Gerry, do you always swallow your pain? Do you always suffer in silence?'

My world blew open.

'**Do you always swallow your pain? Do you always suffer in silence?'**

'Your reaction to the pain,' he continued, 'has been to clench your teeth and your jaw. You have sucked in and you have swallowed your pain. Do you not know the consequences of that? Do you not know the consequences of suppressed emotional pain?'

This was such a profound question.

'For the last five minutes I eased up with the massage and was barely touching you,' he added. 'But even in that light touch you experienced the same pain as the first 10 minutes of our session, despite my contact changing completely. You continued to grip the bed and clench your jaw for the last 5 minutes.

It was like Ravi had hit a nerve – not a physical nerve, but an emotional nerve. He had somehow seen something in me, a tension, a stress, a tightness or a pain that I was holding. He had seen my refusal to admit weakness, vulnerability, my fear of being perceived by others as less than. He could see where in the body I was holding this emotional pain, and as he applied a little bit of pressure to it, he brought my awareness to it. The pain was far more emotional than physical. The first great lesson I learned from Ravi was that somewhere, somehow in my life I had learned to swallow my pain, to suppress it. And in the face of my pain I clenched my jaw, I bit down on my lip and I forced myself through it.

Don't be embarrassed by your pain

Over the rest of the session he got me to breathe deeply, at each moment when the pain would arrive. He got me to have a large exhale and then to chant and scream. I remember how embarrassed I felt as I made those loud roars, as though I had become an animal, screaming. I wondered what the people outside were thinking, what Ravi was thinking about me.

And as I sat in that state of embarrassment, Ravi once again stopped, knelt down beside me and said, 'My dear, why are you embarrassed about your pain? What is so embarrassing about a wounded human being? Are you not the person to whom wounded people come? What do you tell them? Do you tell them to be embarrassed about it, to suppress it, to swallow it up for fear of what other people will think, or do you tell them to express it?' I said I told them to express it. 'Well,' he said, 'it's time to take your own advice.'

The session with Ravi gave me incredible insights into how I handle and hold emotional hurt and pain, about the embarrassment I felt at expressing it. How awkward I could be about vulnerability and how at some level in my subconscious programs there was still a voice saying, *Bottle up, toughen up, man up, get through it.* I realised that part of my emotional default state was shame – shame about my pain, shame that I couldn't fix it myself and shame that I wasn't stronger. I began to realise that I was still carrying a huge amount of unconscious emotion that I was afraid to let surface and that I was dedicating a lot of my time and energy towards keeping those emotions locked away and suppressed.

Press Pause

Think of a time when you experienced an overwhelming wave of emotion. Did you feel embarrassment or shame? Were you embarrassed because you were feeling the emotion or because of the emotion itself? Next time you begin to feel emotional, try to dig a little deeper and ask yourself if you are embarrassed by the feelings and why. Take a few minutes to write or journal about this and see what emerges. Don't judge or analyse what comes onto the page. Simply observe. Be truthful and honest with yourself, holding that inner child dearly within you as you write and record what surfaces with tender grace, ease and love.

With Ravi I began to realise that even the pain we experience in the body can be as much emotional as physical. A deep psychological, emotional or spiritual pain can hurt far more than a physical wound. Sometimes the knots in our shoulders are caused by physical symptoms and other times by emotional suppression. Sometimes the knot in our stomach has nothing to do with the physical – very often it is due to psychological and emotional suppression. A very important step in living with good emotional health is the ability and freedom we give ourselves to feel emotions without resistance and to express them without judgement or embarrassment.

Press Pause

Think of the way we speak to children when they fall or get upset. Generally we try to distract them from their emotions, to stop the upset or take away the emotion. We tell them,

'You're OK. It's just a cut. It's just a tumble. Up you get.'
But what lessons are we giving the child by telling them to
toughen it out and instructing them not to express their
emotions? What lessons were we given as children that we
are still carrying with us? Perhaps we can't show weakness or
ask for help? We need to learn to give ourselves, and others,
safe space to feel our emotions fully.

What the mind suppresses, the body expresses: taking ownership of our emotions and our emotional pain

After having several incredible sessions with Ravi I decided to send one of my clients to him. Let's call my client Michael. Michael had a lot of stress and trauma in his life and, like me, for many years his solution was to bottle it up, toughen up, grind it out. But it was now beginning to have a negative impact on his health and well-being. His body was wracked in pain, in tightness and stiffness. So I sent him to Ravi.

I was eager to find out how he got on, so after I knew the session would have ended I gave him a call. 'That man is dangerous,' he told me, 'and I'm not going back.' I felt bad. This was my client, and I felt 'd let him down. But deep down I knew that maybe this was his chance.

When I was next with Ravi I casually mentioned that I'd sent Michael to see him. Ravi, protecting Michael's confidence, said very little. I told Ravi that Michael found the pain too intense. 'He asked you to ease off,' I said, 'but you didn't.'

Ravi waited a second before replying. 'The pain Michael felt is Michael's pain,' he said. 'The intensity of that pain has nothing to do with me. I simply brought awareness to the pain that Michael is holding and suppressing, and

'**What the mind suppresses, the body expresses.**'

the intensity he felt is simply the intensity of his resistance to it. But now, he has a choice: he can meet it and dissolve it and move it out of the body, or he can continue to suppress it and deny it, leading to deeper pain, until it reaches a point where his physical health breaks down. The pain is caused by his reaction and resistance to his traumas. I simply brought awareness to the pain he is holding. The choice is now his – the responsibility lies not with me but with Michael.'

What the mind suppresses, the body expresses. When we choose to hide our emotional pain, to suppress it, to bottle it up, to grind it out, it has deep and long-lasting consequences for our health and our happiness.

Examples of how suppression of emotions can impact our health include increased stress levels, a weakened immune system, exacerbation of mental health conditions such as anxiety or depression, sleep disturbances, physical symptoms such as headaches, chronic pain and digestive issues, along with relationship difficulties and misunderstandings causing resentment and putting a strain on social connections. If we are feeling tired it is important that we look beyond the physical body for the root cause of that tiredness and ask two important questions:

- Do I always swallow my pain, and if so, why?
- Am I embarrassed by my pain?

It is important to note that our experiences with suppressing emotions can differ, and not all of us will encounter the same effects. However, recognising and addressing our emotions in a healthy manner is vital for our overall well-being.

Press Pause

- *When it comes to emotions, do you give yourself time and space to feel them?*
- *What is your immediate reaction when you feel an unwanted emotion coming up?*
- *Do you ever swallow your emotions?*
- *What is your normal reaction to not being in control?*
- *What is your reaction to being vulnerable?*
- *Do you stop and allow your emotions to surface or do you get busy and distracted in an attempt to outrun them or drown them out?*
- *If you did give yourself the time and freedom to feel your emotions, what would they be? What would be the most important emotion that would surface? What is the root cause of this emotion?*
- *Where might trapped or suppressed emotions be trying to communicate with you in your body or physical health?*
- *What are you tired of suppressing? What are you tired of running from?*

Breaking our addiction to stress chemicals

A very important step in regulating our emotional health is learning how to break our addiction to the chemicals that so many of our emotions create. Emotions like fear, shame, guilt and anger produce chemicals such as cortisol and adrenaline that are released by the brain when we are stressed. If we experience them for long enough, we can become extremely addicted to them; when we don't have them we start to crave them in a self-perpetuating cycle of dependency and negative emotions. In effect we become chemically addicted to feelings of anger and hurt and it becomes a difficult cycle or thought process to break.

Who is the one perpetuating our emotions?
We need to stop poking the bear

When we are in a state of emotional disregulation it's important that we don't get caught in the cycle of creating our own emotional stress simply to get access to the addictive chemicals. It's as if we are poking the sleeping bear; if we stop poking the bear, the bear is happy to sleep, and we don't get hurt. When I catch myself perpetuating my own suffering and negative emotions, I simply tell myself to stop poking the bear. No-one can think in my mind but me and I am the only one who can generate or perpetuate an emotion in me; no-one else can.

Fighting fire with fire is nonsense

It is possible to be internally anxious in a calm external environment, and it is equally possible to be internally calm in an externally anxious or chaotic world. The more we develop good emotional health and strong internal emotional regulation, the more we realise that in a world of increasing unease and uncertainty it is totally possible to live in an internal world of ease, peace and certainty.

We've all heard the expression 'fighting fire with fire'. It's even used as advice: 'You need to fight fire with fire.' It is said so many times that we might even think it is good advice, but in fact it is total and utter nonsense. Firstly, if we are fighting something, it means we don't agree with it or we don't want it. To meet what we don't agree with or what we don't want with more of what we don't want or don't agree with is simply creating more of the same – more of what we don't agree with and more of what we don't want.

Imagine a firefighter spraying more fire through a hose onto a fire thinking they were somehow going to make the situation better. The only thing that helps to fight a fire is water and the only thing that heals anger is kindness; the only thing that helps panic is calmness and the only thing that defeats hate is love. We cannot change our inner or our outer worlds by turning up with more of what we are trying to change. The truth about emotional regulation is that we must become emotionally free from our external situation or environment. We must become emotionally different and more powerful than our past, more powerful than our situation and more powerful than the current environment. We can't change a situation or make it better if our emotions and thinking are the same as the environment that caused them.

Press Pause

Imagine the next time you are in an argument with someone: a loved one or a work colleague or even someone you don't know very well. What is gained by meeting anger head-on? What about if you were to reframe the situation and change your emotion from one of anger and frustration to one of love and peace? This does not mean condemnation or failure; sometimes the greatest and strongest of actions is not anger or rage but deep presence, love, forgiveness, compassion and kindness. If you were to do this, what would the outcome be for you?

Recognising the imaginary threat that comes from within

Emotional health requires us to identify and locate the source of our emotional distress, and very often when we take the time to investigate this we realise that the source of our emotional stress is closer to home than we think.

Have you ever experienced turbulence when flying? If we are in any way a nervous flyer, despite turbulence being a very natural occurrence, it can quickly make us uncomfortable. Within seconds we go from being nice and relaxed to being alert and uneasy, and as well as the turbulence you hear some strange noises coming from the wing of the aircraft. Despite most of us having zero aeronautical engineering qualifications, we can immediately begin to tell ourselves that this isn't normal. Suddenly the bell sounds and the captain instructs passengers to fasten their seatbelts, and at the same time the flight attendant runs past looking very worried. Our brain is processing all these signs and has no choice but to create a story of doom. Our heart starts to race, our hands get sweaty, our rate of breathing increases and before long we are wondering if we should phone our families to say goodbye. We begin to feel increased fear and anger and we ask ourselves why the pilot isn't doing something about it, as if by some miracle we have suddenly just qualified as a pilot and we now know more than they do. In a state of fear, the ego, always trying to protect us, wants to lash out at someone or something, wants to project our fear and anger outwards. As the turbulence continues for what seems like forever, we begin to prepare for the worst. Our brains and our emotions can have us dead and buried on nothing more than a few external cues and an internal story that often has very little to do with reality.

Then suddenly the turbulence stops, the flight attendant walks past with a hot sandwich and the brain switches off alarm mode and we begin to see reality. The turbulence lasted three minutes, it is perfectly normal, and the noise we heard was the landing gear coming down. The seatbelt sign came on as it always does to get people back into their seats to prepare for landing and the flight attendant with the panic on his face had remembered that someone had ordered a toasted sandwich and he was running to get it before landing. And while we were in a state of anxiety, the pilots were sitting in the cockpit relaxed, chatting about the TV programme they had watched last night, in full knowledge that everything was perfectly normal and under control.

In that moment we created our own suffering, and the chemical and physiological changes that happened in our nervous system and our brain were switched on by nothing other than our self-created internal dialogue. Our sympathetic nervous system and our emotional stress response was brought on by thought alone.

And what about when the threat is more emotional – a situation where our unconscious emotional wounds are touched, where our deepest beliefs, values and inner stories are challenged? The thinking self, or the ego, reacts in the same way. We immediately begin to operate from our sympathetic nervous system – our response to the situation is fight (challenge the source of the perceived threat) or flight (run away).

When it comes to emotional threats, switching on our fight-or-flight response is easy as it is a learned and automatic response that can happen instantly. Switching it off and switching on our recovery, the parasympathetic nervous system, is not as easy but we can learn how to do it and will look at this in more detail in the section 'The Emotional Choice'. The issue is that many of us either don't know how or, if we do, we forget to do it in heightened situations. This means that we can spend extended periods of time living in the emotions of stress and fear, even long after the threat has disappeared.

Press Pause

Imagine this scenario: tomorrow morning, you are due to travel for work. You've done this trip numerous times but today you begin to feel nervous about missing the flight or the flight being delayed. You're worried that you haven't prepared enough for the day of meetings. You feel anxious and stressed about something that's not even happening in the present moment. Your emotional reaction to the imagined events triggers responses in your body – anxiety, stress, shame – as though the missed flight has actually happened. The next time you feel yourself reacting to a situation, maybe it's worth really questioning things: what facts do you have? Is the threat real or coming from something that you believe to be true? What if that belief wasn't true? Knowing what you know now, can you begin to change your emotional reaction?

A state of personality

If we stay in an emotional state for a few hours it's just a state; if we stay in it for a longer period it becomes our mood; and if we stay in it long enough it becomes our personality. How many times have you heard someone ask, 'What is he angry about?' and the answer is, 'Nothing, he is just an angry person.' Or how many times have you heard, 'He is a negative person'? Deep down we know these are not actually things we are born with.

They are things we have learned, they are emotions we switched on for some reason and we never switched them off, and for many we don't even know how to switch them off. And we have spent so long in this emotional state we begin to believe the lie that 'this is just the way I am'. It may be the way you are right now but it absolutely does not have to be.

'If we stay in an emotional state for a few hours it's just a state; if we stay in it for a longer period it becomes our mood; and if we stay in it long enough it becomes our personality.'

The amount of time we spend in an emotional state has massive implications for our health and happiness. The stress we experience in the moment of an attack, like a gazelle being attacked by a lion, is acute stress and is a natural and normal response, but the stress we experience over a longer period is called chronic stress. This is why it is so important to be able to identify our emotional triggers, to switch off our sympathetic nervous system, to become more conscious of our emotions so that we can come to our emotional edge and dissolve unhelpful unconscious emotions.

How we store emotions

We store emotions in two ways: we can store them consciously, where we are aware of them, or unconsciously, where we are not aware of them. Both conscious and unconscious emotions can be caused by the presence of something or the absence of something.

Conscious (temporary) emotional state

Our conscious or temporary emotional state is when we experience an emotional reaction through the presence of a stimulus or as a direct consequence of an external event, a piece of information, a piece of news, something we are actively focused on or an inner narrative that is currently running in our minds. It's the type of emotion that is directly linked to something that is happening or something that has happened or something we think is about to happen. We may be feeling emotions of joy, love and peace and then a phone call, an email, a text message might change that emotion into one of sadness, envy, grief or regret. This is normal and this is part of life.

Remarkably, the physiological aspects of emotions are very short-lived experiences. Dr Jill Bolte Taylor has written about the 90 second rule which shows that it takes 90 seconds for the chemicals – adrenaline, cortisol, dopamine and oxytocin – released by the brain to flush out of the body. It's when we interfere with these emotions that they linger. What can seem to be a lasting emotion caused by one event is actually a series of correlating and perpetuating emotional reactions that continue long after the actual event. The thing keeping the emotion going is our inner stories and beliefs. It's these unconscious and unprocessed emotions which have the most influence on our emotional health.

Unconscious emotional state

Our unconscious emotional state is driven by the emotions we have experienced in our lives and are now holding unconsciously. These are the emotions that we carry and have carried for quite a period of time, and they are primarily associated with our past, our traumas (presence), our memories, our deepest beliefs (presence), our unmet emotional needs and our emotional hurts (absence of attachment and love), and they can have a deep impact on our everyday life, affecting both our health and our happiness. Our unconscious emotional state, and our deeply held beliefs are the two key factors which affect our reactions to all situations, stimuli and events happening around and to us.

Learning about our unconscious emotional state is essential so that we are better able to navigate our temporary emotional state. Our unconscious emotions drive us in our everyday life and impact both our health and our sense of well-being. They are the lens through which we see the world. The unconscious emotional state that we all carry informs the way in which we react to temporary emotions, and this is what we need to learn to regulate, change and control in order to achieve lasting inner peace.

Understanding our emotional state

Our emotional state can be defined as combinations of physiological, chemical and thinking activities that create changes in our mood, our mental clarity and our physical sensations.

Sometimes emotions can be felt as uncomfortable and difficult, and sometimes we wish we didn't have to feel them. However, if there were no emotions as the stimuli of feelings, nothing could ever hurt us, but nor would we be able to feel love, joy or excitement, or appreciate the good things life has to offer. In order to begin accessing good emotional health, we need to be able to read emotions without judgement. But first we must understand why we feel the way we do and why we react emotionally in different ways to different stimuli, real, imagined or memorised. All emotions point to something important: they let us know when something is right or isn't right. They can act as a great signpost or inner compass that shows us when we are out of balance, when we are denying our true being. They can let us know if and when we are suppressing our dreams and if we are holding onto old hurts and traumas.

Our emotional state can be impacted by the absence or the presence of something

Most people can identify the things that are impacting their emotional state. It is easy to see that our emotional state can be impacted by the presence of something – a physical threat, a threatening inner narrative, a trauma – but we must also be aware that our emotional state can be impacted by the absence of something.

Very often, whether we are aware of it or not, we can be in a state of emotional disregulation when there is nothing visible or tangible to cause this. If there isn't the presence of something then the chances are that our emotional disregulation is being caused by the absence of a deeper emotional need that has never been met or has been denied. This can be the absence of secure emotional attachment, emotional safety or emotional consistency, or it can be unmet emotional needs.

The absence of a primary emotional need

For many people, emotional needs can be similar – for example, the need to feel safe, the need to be seen, the need to be unconditionally loved, the need to be acknowledged, the need to be held and to experience loving human touch and the need to be connected and to feel part of something bigger than ourselves.

The need to feel safe is a primary need. If any of us grew up in an environment where we didn't feel safe, where there was hostility or uncertainty in our home, our entire nervous system may feel out of balance, making us operate from a place of fear. This can take us out of a place of peace and safety and take our nervous system into a place of consistent fight or flight. Until we get these emotional needs met, our nervous system and our psyche or soul will stay in a place of fear.

To grow up in a hostile or unpredictable environment, with parents who are emotionally unstable, whether within themselves or in their relationships, can have huge implications.

When our primary emotional need for security and safety is not met, we experience this as trauma – energetically, mentally and physically, as all of these human systems are interconnected. All emotional trauma creates a physical trauma as the nervous system fires the sympathetic mode and we are flooded with the chemicals and hormones of stress and survival. If unresolved, this sympathetic mode becomes the default mode of our central nervous system and we can spend our entire adult lives operating in high stress, always scanning for the next crisis, believing the world is unsafe and uncertain.

Attachment is an essential human need, and one of the most powerful. In fact, no mammalian species can survive without attachment; only a reptile can do so. If our need for attachment is not met, it will negatively impact our happiness, our health, our well-being and our ability to form long-lasting, loving relationships in the future, as we operate from a place of fear that we are not enough or that we have to earn love. Learning to trust others, learning to have clear boundaries, understanding our emotional needs and learning to regulate ourselves in deep relationships is a vital skill if we are to form healthy and happy relationships. Knowing our attachment styles is also very important as this level of self-understanding is crucial when it comes to how we find and create loving relationships.

Attachment is described as the way in which we seek and receive love. It is our inner blueprint that helps us manage ourselves, our relationships with others and our emotions as we navigate through the dynamics of human life.

Understanding emotional attachment

Every human being has a deep emotional need for acceptance, safety and love. Love involves a two-way feeling – both feeling loved and being loveable. It is essential that this need is met in order for us to have secure attachment with the world, with ourselves and with other people. Secure attachment gives us the emotional ability to form healthy, loving relationships where we

'Every human being has a deep emotional need for acceptance, safety and love.'

can be devoted and committed to our partner but never totally dependent on or at the mercy of their actions. With a secure attachment mode we can be interdependent and we do not have to be dependent on another person. But most importantly, secure attachment allows us to love ourselves as we are, fully and completely. The absence of this has a profound effect on our unconscious emotional state and how we react to external stimuli throughout our lives.

The emotional need of psychological safety

A second important primary emotional need is the need to not have to work for our attachment needs to be met, and to feel safe as we express ourselves in our truest form. When I work with high-performance teams or corporate teams one of the first and most important things we need to establish and consistently foster and nourish is psychological and emotional safety. Psychological and emotional safety is the knowledge and certainty that you won't be punished, isolated or emotionally bullied for expressing your true self or for speaking up with your questions, concerns, ideas and feelings. Anyone who is part of a team knows the importance of this and the power it has to create real and solid relationships when it is fostered, and to shatter trust, confidence and connection when it is not.

Unconditional love does not have to be earned

The same applies to family or a family dynamic. As infants and young children we should not feel that we have to work to be accepted or to be loved. When we can be in a relationship where we feel safe and at ease, without the need to work, this allows our body, our brain, our nervous system to rest and recover and allows the parts of our brain associated with calmness and emotional control to become bigger and stronger.

If we grew up in an environment where our parents were in a state of emotional unrest, or emotional disregulation, we would have to work hard to fight that state of disregulation in our attempts to secure further attention, affection and connection. This sense of having to fight against the disregulation of our parents' emotional state or having to somehow overcome the emotional disregulation in the relationship between our parents creates an overactive limbic brain, an overactive stress-based sympathetic central nervous system and emotional state where we are always working hard to try to establish a connection, a sense of safety and a sense of love.

This leads to deep psychological beliefs that we are only loved, safe or accepted when we work, achieve, behave or perform in a certain way – we feel we need to earn the attachment we are seeking.

When we look at our own emotional unrest, when we examine the state of our own central nervous system, it is useful to look back and ask ourselves certain questions. What was the state of emotional regulation that I experienced? What was the state of emotional regulation that I experienced from my parents? What was the emotional connection and regulation in the home? What was the emotional state of the relationship between my parents?

If it feels like you were a soldier growing up in an unpredictable, unstable environment, then don't be surprised if, just like a soldier after returning from war, you have developed some version of an underlying anxiety state where your post-traumatic stress is actually current traumatic stress because of the trauma of the past and the unmet emotional needs. In fact, I would say that the trauma is ongoing and will be until you have met and addressed those needs in a healthy way.

The capacity to feel our emotions to the full without fear of rejection or negative consequence is an essential human emotional need. If a child experiences, at some point, an inability to express all their emotions, or if their emotions or emotional reactions are frowned upon, then that child, craving acceptance from its tribe, will begin to suppress those emotions. If as a child you were told to be brave, to stop crying, you might feel that showing emotion is a negative thing, a sign of weakness. As an adult, you might have problems communicating your true feelings for fear that they might be dismissed or reduced. In order to achieve emotional stability and regulation, greater balance, coherence and emotional health, it is imperative that we regain the trust, confidence, courage and skills to express our emotional needs.

> 'The capacity to feel our emotions to the full without fear of rejection or negative consequence is an essential human emotional need.'

PEOPLE-PLEASING: AN UNDERCURRENT OF UNCONSCIOUS EMOTIONS

People-pleasing is another powerful example of how deep-rooted unconscious emotions can be made visible in everyday living. Unfortunately, very often our emotional expression can be blocked by our caregivers, our peers or the society in which we live. Consequently, we might only express the emotions we feel will get us accepted and loved, and suppress the rest. When we have a strong need to be liked, to be loved, to be accepted, we will suppress all emotions and all emotional reactions that might put this in jeopardy. People-pleasing is an adaptation method. It is a coping mechanism developed by people who have been emotionally suppressed and who fear that if they were to express themselves in their truest form, they would somehow be rejected.

Many of us as adults are still not able to truly demand or name our emotional needs. Very often we are working in a job that doesn't serve us and our soul is trying to tell us it wants something more but we stay in it; we have a dream to be free to travel, but we cling to the safe, secure job. Often we stay in a relationship that doesn't nourish us. So many of us are constantly giving our time and attention to other people and we are trying to fit ourselves into whatever space is left when everybody else's needs are met. Very often this means that there is simply no space for our emotional needs to be met. Unmet emotional needs leave a void, a space. They leave an uneasiness, an unhappiness and a sense of dissatisfaction, a feeling that we are less than. A sense of restlessness and that something is off-kilter.

The problem for many of us is that we are so busy, so distracted, we can't even listen to the physical needs of the body let alone the emotional needs of our soul and this results in emotional dis-health. Very often the body is craving sleep, but instead we just give it coffee. Very often the body is craving that we slow down, but we just go faster and tell ourselves to push through. Very often we are eating food that we know is hurting the body, but we keep eating it.

If we can't even listen to our own body, if we can't listen to our own central nervous system, how can we listen to and identify our deepest emotional needs to begin to live with better emotional health? And if we can't identify them, how do we even begin to meet them?

Healing the inability to name emotional needs without the fear of rejection

We are all different, and we will all have individual emotional needs. For some people the emotional need of freedom is really important; for others it's the emotional need of security and predictability. For some the emotional need of creativity and self-expression is what is key. Different people have different needs that are highly individual and specific and unique to that person. When we are growing up, if our emotional needs are not met,

'We are all different, and we will all have individual emotional needs.'

it leaves an absence, a void, a hole in which we are constantly craving; we are constantly trying to find something to fill this inner void. The danger as adults is that we try to fill these needs in other ways, often through addiction to food, alcohol, social media, work, external affirmation, recognition and even exercise.

When we do not honour these needs, or listen to them or align with them for whatever reason, we begin to lose the ability to recognise the vital role they play in maintaining our health and happiness. It is really important that we begin to truly value our needs, our desires, our birthright requirements, and to cherish them with a sense of worthiness and pride. By doing so, it will enable us to honour these needs and show up for ourselves without having guilt or the fear of rejection. Later we will explore more on this topic and how to set emotional boundaries for greater inner peace, ease and mental health.

Press Pause

Ask yourself the question: What are my deep emotional needs?
The need to be seen, to be heard, to be loved? To feel valued and to feel safe?
Then ask yourself: When do I feel happiest? When do I feel safest? When do I feel most whole and at peace? Then look at those instances and see if they have anything in common. Begin to identify what your emotional needs are. Do you have a deep-seated need for security? Is it for adventure and discovery? Then begin to live your life fulfilling those needs.

The presence of trauma

As mentioned above, it can be the presence of something that leads to emotional dis-health – for example, the presence of a past trauma can have a very powerful impact on our emotional state. Although the trauma may have happened a long time ago, unless we have successfully and completely dissolved and healed it the emotional impact of it may still be present. The word 'trauma' comes from the Greek word for 'wound'. Trauma is a constriction, a diminishment in our psychological, emotional and physiological functioning. Trauma is not about what happens to us: it is about what happens inside of us in response to what happens to us.

When we go through trauma our brains and nervous systems shift into survival mode. Like a deer trying to avoid an oncoming high-speed car, our brains direct all our mental and physical energy towards dealing with the immediate threat until it's gone.

Trauma mainly affects three important parts of our brain. The amygdala is our emotional and instinctual centre; when a person experiences a traumatic event, adrenaline rushes through the body and the memory is imprinted into the amygdala, which is part of the limbic system. The amygdala holds the emotional significance of the event, including the intensity and impulse of emotion. Trauma also impacts the hippocampus, which controls memory; trauma leads to reduced activity in the hippocampus, one of whose functions is to distinguish between past and present, and this is another reason why we can get trapped in a perpetuating traumatic response long after the actual trauma has passed, as our brain can't tell the difference between the actual traumatic event and the memory of it. This is why even the memory of a trauma can be experienced as a trauma in itself, or how any person or experience that reminds us of a traumatic experience can cause an emotional reaction that is disproportionate to what is actually happening. Trauma can cause the brain to remain in a state of hypervigilance, suppressing memory and impulse control and trapping us in a constant state of strong emotional reactivity. Trauma also inhibits the prefrontal cortex, which is responsible for regulating emotions and impulses. This means that if we have unresolved trauma, we lose the ability to bring reasoning, logic or perspective into the picture.

Sometimes, our initial trauma response does not get turned off, making it difficult for us to function and experience normal levels of happiness and health. Trauma can change the way we think, feel and act for a long time after the actual trauma has ended. For many people, this could mean flashbacks or nightmares, a constant feeling of being on edge, loneliness, anger or other destructive emotions.

The ongoing state where the brain and body are trapped in an ever-present activation of the trauma response is often called the frozen present. We are almost frozen in time, where our brain, our body and our nervous system are trapped, thinking the trauma is happening over and over again. This can result in a constant feeling of anxiety and uneasiness where we are in the fight-or-flight state and it can also lead to feelings of numbness where we are trapped in the freeze state. Traumas can be the events that we instinctively think of, bereavement, car accidents and so on, but they can be also the smaller moments that are less stand-out. They can be the accumulation of lots of little failings and setbacks, an accumulation of times we felt not good enough, moments where we expected our parents to be there and they weren't, moments where we were exposed to adults or family members in states of emotional disregulation.

For a brain to function in a healthy way and to its optimum ability, all its parts need to communicate, from the bottom of the brain to the upper parts of the higher brain. There must be consistent and strong communication between the left and right sides of the brain. When the lower part of the brain responsible for survival is repeatedly activated through trauma or an insecure environment or insecure attachment in infancy and in early childhood, this can reduce the connections between other parts of the brain. Consequently, it can significantly impact our ability to learn, to form memories, to regulate emotions, and can affect our ability to be calm, to think, to reflect and to respond flexibly and in a planned way.

Emotional trauma, which is deep fear, overwhelm, sadness, anxiety, anger, which is held in the body, can cause physical symptoms years later such as headaches, jumpiness, chronic pain and dissociation. When we have an overwhelming experience, our logical mind might feel 'over it' before our body does.

We all know the bigger events of trauma like war, a plane crash, a house fire or a traffic accident but we can also be traumatised by our relationships, our relations with others and with ourselves. For me, with all my life experience and learnings, I deeply believe the biggest and most hurtful trauma a human being can experience is the feeling of being unloved or unloveable. Trauma that wounds our soul, trauma that slowly erodes our self-esteem, trauma that leaves us feeling not good enough, the little traumas that are happening slowly that no one sees, can be so damaging.

Trauma is of course often the presence of something but now I hope we begin to realise that trauma can also be the absence of something, and the absence of an emotional need or the constant abandoning of our own emotional needs, where we are either too distracted to know them or too afraid to name and demand them. Trauma can be deeply felt if we are constantly neglecting our deepest needs, and by abandoning our deepest needs we are abandoning our true self and by doing so we are taking our soul away from its place of peace.

The presence of a belief system

The things that stir up the most powerful emotions in us are the beliefs we hold. A belief is something that we hold to be true about ourselves, about other people, about the world or about all these things. A belief can be founded in scientific and objective fact or it can be founded in a subjective knowing, an inner intuition.

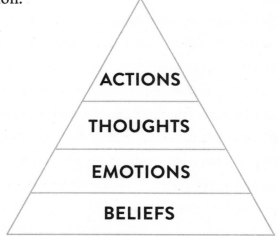

Think of a triangle with four floors or levels in it, all equal in size. On the top floor I want you to put Actions. Actions are the things we do, the big and little things, each and every day. They can be as simple as choosing to take the same route to work every day even though we know we are going to get stuck in traffic, but fear of finding a new way keeps us choosing that same route; or it could be more important like not applying for a new job, not walking up to the beautiful-looking person in the coffee shop and saying hello, not leaving a job that we dislike. All of these actions are never just based on fresh air: they are all based on something deeper.

We can at times believe that we do things without thinking, or for no reason, but there is always a reason. We might do them without conscious thought, but in order for us to act there must be at least an unconscious thought or intention. Actions are driven by conscious or unconscious thoughts or inner narratives, and it is these thoughts that make up the second level of the triangle.

So let's look into the next level of the triangle and see what is driving those thoughts and inner narratives. Our emotions are actually driving so many of our thoughts and our inner narratives, and we know that it is very hard to think outside our emotional state – for example, it's very hard to have happy thoughts if we feel emotionally angry or sad. Neuroscience is showing how our thoughts are greatly shaped by our emotions and that the thoughts we focus on are the ones that are directly in alignment with our emotions.

So far in our triangle we have our actions sitting at the very top, and just underneath we have our thoughts that are driving our actions, and just underneath our thoughts we have our emotions. We still have one floor of the triangle to fill and it's the foundation of all the other floors. The question is what drives our emotions? The obvious answer is the outside world, other people, situations. And yes, these absolutely can and do trigger and play a role in our emotions and our emotional state. But there is something else, something more powerful than the outside world that is driving most of our emotions.

It is our beliefs – beliefs about ourselves, what is happening in the outside world, about why people are saying the things they are and acting the way they are, beliefs about how things will work out. These have more power over our emotional state than anything else in the universe. Our beliefs may be founded in reality, they may be founded in part reality and they may be founded in zero reality. In fact, I have come to realise that most human beings at times hold beliefs about themselves, about other people and about the world that have absolutely zero grounding in reality, and these beliefs can be enabling and life-giving or they can be disabling and destructive. If our emotional and attachment needs were met as a child, this will most likely lead to the presence of a more positive belief system about ourselves and the world. These can be beliefs such as:

- I am capable
- I am strong
- Life isn't always predictable and doesn't have to be

- I do not always have to be in control
- I am free to express my true self
- My emotional needs are valid
- I have the inner confidence and resilience to meet and thrive within adversity

If our needs weren't met, we can believe:
- The world is a cruel place.
- Only the strong survive.
- Vulnerability is a weakness.
- Nice people don't win.
- I am not deserving.
- I am not born for greatness.
- Big opportunities don't happen to me or rarely happen.
- If people saw the real me they wouldn't like me.
- My success is linked to my productivity.
- It's important that I fit in.
- It's my role to make other people happy.
- It's not right to challenge others.
- It's selfish to demand my emotional needs.
- It's hard to meet people to fall in love with.
- I am unlucky in relationships.
- I am not as clever as other people.

Where do our beliefs come from?

In order to become our true selves and be able to truly follow our own path, it is very important that we stop to think about how many of our deepest beliefs, limitations, expectations and unconscious biases have actually been downloaded by us from other people.

From the age of zero to eight we are operating on a very specific brain wave called a theta brain wave. This allows us to learn information, language, social cues and so on at an extremely fast pace. It is such an effective learning frequency that it means we are literally downloading everything we see, everything we experience and are exposed to. The only downside is that, because we are downloading so fast, the information is being submitted to our subconscious mind before we have the ability to pass it through our logical brain, which means we literally submit and believe everything without any logical filter. We know that 90 per cent of our subconscious beliefs are in place by the age of eight.

The beliefs of our tribes

Tribes are essential to the flourishing of human beings. We are social beings, and we are tied into the tribe. At the very beginning, when human beings appeared on Earth, the planet was inhabited by big, dangerous animals. So in order for us to thrive and succeed, in order for us to survive, we had a better chance when we were together in numbers. In order to stay in a tribe, we had to be loved by the tribe – we had to be accepted and needed by the tribe, and therefore it was important that we held the same belief systems as the tribe. If the tribe felt that it didn't need us, or love us, if we showed a weakness, or if the tribe thought we didn't have value or worth, we were left behind, which was a terrifying place to be. Having a different belief system could be a very dangerous thing, as social acceptance was more important than self-expression, and so we took on the beliefs of the tribe – and maybe never even questioned them – in the pursuit of fitting in and not the pursuit of truth.

This is still in the human psyche and this is why, at times, we are afraid to show vulnerability, we are afraid to be seen as weak, we are afraid if we don't have a value, if we don't have a contribution to make, if we're not loved or needed we will be left behind. It's why we fear exclusion so much. We have a deep need to feel included and accepted. And so we will do everything and anything to stay in the tribe, and accepting the tribe's beliefs is a way of becoming part of it and fitting in with it. Deep within the human psyche is an undercurrent, a powerful need to be loved, to be seen, to be needed and to have a purpose, and this need will overpower every other need, especially the need for individual expression and individual beliefs. That's why we begin to replicate the accents, the mannerisms, the habits and the beliefs of the people around us. We need them to know we are one of them and part of their tribe, we accept what they accept and believe in what they believe, and we will even download and accept their beliefs about us. Sometimes this can be our interpretation of their beliefs about us – because of the things they say to us or the things they do to us we can arrive at conclusions about how our family and our tribe feel about us and what they believe about us. And these conclusions may or may not be founded in reality.

Most people, when exposed to very different sets of beliefs or norms, can quickly reject the new ones as a way of protecting and staying affiliated to their original tribe and their original sense of identity, security and belonging. This can be especially strong with family beliefs, as our family is often our first and most immediate tribe, and this is why to be rejected by them can be so painful and why so many people sacrifice their own beliefs and expressions in order to stay with in those of their family, and we begin to play the roles within our family that make us feel accepted, needed or loved.

The beliefs and subconscious programs we hold go on to shape so much of our life, including the person we become, along with our emotional responses. That's why it is so important that we not only examine our deepest beliefs and programs on a regular basis but are also always willing to accept that even our most deeply held beliefs – about ourselves and the world – may not be true.

We often come to know so much about ourselves through the people in our lives rather than through our own inner reflection; we become what people say we are or what they want or need us to be. We can often download their ideas, beliefs and expectations of us and when we do we unconsciously fall into the role that fulfils these beliefs and expectations.

The more our emotional health, the more our feelings of safety, meaning, love and worth are connected to other people, the more we lose the ability to self-regulate our emotional well-being. We are social beings and of course being in healthy relationships is really important, but healthy relationships are the ones that allow us to be ourselves. They are not relationships where our emotional well-being is dependent on others. Think of a healthy forest: in order for a forest to be strong each individual tree must be strong in itself, with its own

> 'The more our emotional health, the more our feelings of safety, meaning, love and worth are connected to other people, the more we lose the ability to self-regulate our emotional well-being'

strong roots and its own ability to grow as high as it wants. Relationships are similar: a relationship is only healthy when all people in that relationship are emotionally healthy.

So many of our beliefs, expectations and roles are unconscious; they can often lead to a disconnect or an unhealthy thread that weaves people together in a relationship that is forced because the expectations and beliefs have never actually been spoken about openly or agreed. Nowhere is this more evident than in family dynamics and in our relationships with other people.

Relationships between all human beings can be complex, and in order to navigate them successfully we need at times to step back and look at human interactions and human dynamics and human relationships and see what exactly they are and what underpins them. Humans beings are dynamic beings, which means we're always changing, and always growing. We are meant to regularly check in with and change our belief systems, re-evaluate what's important, change the things we attach ourselves to, but as we move through our lives we can neglect to do this and this can create feelings of restlessness, unfulfillment and unhappiness. And as a result, our emotional health will be negatively affected.

While all human relationships and dynamics are important, one of the most important is family dynamics. There is no doubt that our families can be our greatest gift – our greatest support and source of love, inspiration and confidence – and often our greatest emotional challenge. This is because they are our primary caregivers, our primary tribe, a place in which, in our early years as children, we were meant to experience feelings of safety, comfort and connection. If we don't experience these things, we can begin to think that there is something wrong with us. We feel rejected and we can spend the rest of our adult lives trying to find this emotional connection and acceptance we yearned for as a child – all the while holding an unconscious belief that, until we get this level of acceptance and connection, there's something wrong with us.

Depending on the family unit, depending on the family dynamic, very often the family can be the hardest place from which to get inspiration or confidence or self-esteem, and our family can be the place of our greatest emotional triggers.

The role I play and should play in relationships

If our emotional health is connected or attached to feeling accepted by others, we will look to take on a role that makes us feel accepted, even if that role means supressing or denying our own emotional needs.

One of the biggest identity pillars we develop, and from

which we get our attention and affection, is the role we play in the family. It is hugely important and is why when many of us start to play such a role from the beginning of our life – it could be the peacemaker or the problem-solver – we become so accustomed to it that we continue to play it in every relationship for the rest of our lives. It is therefore very important to look at the role we play in our families. What is the role I've always played? And when I go home to my family, even as an adult, do I find myself playing the same role, going back into the same space and beginning to feel and think the same way I always did growing up?

Think of the role you play in your relationship. Are you able to name and ask for your emotional needs to be met or are you the problem-solver, the fixer, the peacekeeper, the backseat driver, the one in the shadows, the one who always puts everyone else's needs first? We might tell ourselves that this is because we are caring and loving – maybe it is, or maybe it is because we have been conditioned to be like this, to suppress our own emotional needs, to deny our own unhappiness. Maybe there is another way to look at this. Maybe we do all these things so that we are wanted and needed and as long as we are wanted and needed we will not be rejected. Far too many people fall into this trap of being the servant of the relationship and can become angry or bitter towards the other person but never really ask for or demand a different role and so their partner never really knows. Are you playing roles that no longer serve you? Would you like to break free from these roles?

The invisible force of family dynamics: shaping our unconscious emotions

Family dynamics are what primarily shape our unconscious emotional state. The family dynamic is the undercurrent of our unconscious programs, the undercurrent of our need to be seen and to be loved. It is the primary place where we are given the self-love, self-acceptance, self-esteem and self-confidence to step bravely into the world – or not.

Every morning as part of my routine, I go for a run along the harbour close to where we live. And I am always taken by the same thing – all the sailing boats floating in the water are always facing identically in the same direction. Line by line, boat by boat, each perfectly aligned with the next, at the exact same angle, in perfect symmetry. It's as if someone has come along in the night and aligned each and every boat. Now of course we know that is not what happens: it is the wind that aligns the boats, the boats are simply responding to the wind. As the wind changes, so do the boats. But if we didn't know about the wind, we would be curious as to why all the boats are aligned in the same direction.

The wind that aligns the boats is an invisible field. It is not always forceful, it is often gentle, but it is there and it is always directing the boats as they float in the harbour. This invisible force that has every boat aligned in the same direction is the same as the energy that fills the home in which we grow up. We all grew up in a home and in that home was a mum or dad or brother or sister, maybe grandparents, all different people, and yet in that house the dynamics of that family, the dynamics of certain relationships, the unconscious beliefs of the people in the home, the trauma experienced by the various people in that home creates a force, creates an energy field, creates an atmosphere, creates an invisible presence that we live in and are impacted by each and every day.

As we grow up in that environment, just like the wind shapes the direction of the boats, that invisible force in our homes has a powerful impact on shaping the direction of our deepest beliefs, our emotional expressions, the regulation or disregulation of our nervous systems and the inherited intergenerational trauma that we experience as we live there.

What is preventing us from breaking free of unhelpful beliefs?

Our ego clings to our deepest beliefs – many of which become unhelpful and no longer relevant as we move through life – as if they are true and fixed, but often they are neither.

As we will examine in the next section, 'The Awareness Shift', the human ego is committed to one job, and that is to keep us alive, and the way it does that is by keeping us committed to living in the predictable future based on the remembered past. It will keep us away from the things that hurt us in the past and it will keep us away from anything it sees as a potential place of hurt. But the ego confuses change with danger; it isn't committed to excellence or even happiness: it is simply committed to short-term survival and keeping us trapped in the feelings and emotions of short-term survival. The ego is always ready to fight anything or anyone that challenges our deepest beliefs and behaviours and it will even fight ourselves the moment we begin to change for the better. If our past is full of sadness, disappointment and feelings of not being enough, and if these emotions are familiar to the ego, then the ego, committed to familiarity, will become addicted to these feelings and will fight anything that will change or has the potential to change them; no matter what happens, our ego will find a way of bringing us back to these feelings of disappointment, regret and not being enough.

In 'The Awareness Shift', we will look at practical ways we can begin to become more aware of our ego and how we can begin to control it. From my years of study, life experience and work with clients, I see dissolving the ego, quietening its voice and reducing the role it plays in our lives, our decisions and our happiness, as one of the most important things we can do.

Our beliefs about what life should be can often cause us emotional distress

The deep truth is that there is no contract with life. There is no contract for how long we should live, or the happiness we should enjoy, or the love we should find, or the children we should have. Yet we live with deeply held beliefs and expectations about these things, and when life goes in a different direction than our beliefs, we suffer. We live a life where the word 'should' comes up all too often: *she should know better, she is*

'There is no contract for how long we should live, or the happiness we should enjoy, or the love we should find, or the children we should have.'

my sister, she should care; he is my dad, he should have been there for me; life should be easy, I should be married, I should be able to have children, I shouldn't have to face this.

I have come to realise that because of all these unjustified expectations – where we have deeply held beliefs and imaginary contracts with life and other people – when people don't live up to our imaginary 'shoulds' we suffer: not because of other people's actions or life's situations but because these things do not match the inner beliefs we hold; they do not match the contract that never existed. There are no contracts, not with other people, not with life and not with the universe, but there is a contract we make with ourselves and that is either a freedom contract or an imprisonment contract, a happiness contract or a suffering contract.

I have now become aware that the emotions I experienced on the day of the publication of *Awaken Your Power Within*, as described in the introduction to this book, were to do with the beliefs I held. The truth was that the silence I perceived to be coming from my family that day was simply because they were busy at work, picking up kids, getting to the shop to buy the book. They were busy doing other things but I superimposed my own beliefs about the silence: that I was a bad person, that I was a burden to my parents. Had I not held those beliefs or had I held different beliefs I would have had a different emotional response. I would have known that everyone was simply getting on with their daily lives. It was then I realised the incredible work I still needed to do to really examine my beliefs about the beliefs my family held about me and the emotional importance that I attached to this. I realised that my emotional state and my ability to be emotionally free were still clouded by some self-created belief that I needed to deconstruct and let go.

This was my greatest awakening. It hit me like a flash of light. Life doesn't get easier, the challenges don't get smaller, things don't become fairer, my family doesn't need to change. But I can get stronger and become more free. And for that to happen, my beliefs, my inner compass and my values need to be based on what I truly hold to be true and dear, on my expectations of me and not other people. But bigger than this, I need to alter my belief that the universe is somehow out to get me, alter it to a belief that the universe is either neutral or is actually trying to help me. It is time to get out of fight and striving and into ease and thriving.

OUR BELIEFS ABOUT OURSELVES THAT MIGHT BE HARMING US:

1. I am not enough.
2. I am not deserving.
3. I need to earn love.
4. My opinions don't matter.
5. I need to hide my true self.
6. I need other people's approval to feel validated.
7. It's wrong for me to say no to people.

The emotional shadows we cast

There is a concept I use with my clients that I call 'The shadows we cast'. This again refers to the undercurrent of unconscious emotions that we can often cast out into the world unbeknownst to ourselves. The shadows we cast refers to the environment to which we contribute. As we know now, every one of us has a set of unconscious programs, deeply held beliefs, past traumas and unresolved emotions, and every one of us expresses our emotions in different ways. But the way in which we handle and express these has an impact not just on ourselves, but also on the people around us. Our emotions and our emotional state is being transmitted beyond ourselves and is being picked up and experienced by everyone around us. Just as we can all be impacted by the invisible forces in family dynamics, it is important that we are aware that we are emitting an invisible force and that very often people can be disempowered and even hurt by the emotional shadows we cast.

When I worked with an international Olympic boxing team, we had one boxer who hated training camps. He hated being away from home and regularly became angry and frustrated. At the end of each day we held a team meeting and he often came in and spent 15 to 20 minutes shouting and complaining and pointing out everything that was wrong with the training camp and expressing all his frustrations. This was great for him, this was his way of expressing and unloading, and once he had said it all, he would leave happy and lighter. The problem was everybody else left heavier and less motivated. He had developed a way of expressing his emotions that helped him but was disabling those around him.

Every single one of us must be aware that the way in which we emotionally show up in our marriage, in our home, in our workplace, the energy we bring, the words we use, the things we say, all have a massive impact on the environment and people around us. It's as though we cast a shadow. And that shadow can be full of light and can be uplifting; it can be full of inspiration and joy. Or it can be full of fear, anger and judgement; it may be helpful to you but it may be hurtful to others.

As we were growing up, many of us existed within a shadow, a shadow cast by our parents, a shadow cast by the relationship between our parents, a shadow cast by the sibling who took all the attention, who created all the noise, a shadow cast by a death in the family, a shadow cast by a mental health problem or addiction, a shadow cast by a family member who didn't have the ability to regulate emotions. There can be multiple types of shadows and all can have a massive impact on our emotional health and our emotional development.

The first thing to do is examine the shadow we cast – the way we handle stress, the way we handle emotions, the emotions we are suppressing – and recognise that while it may be helpful to us, we must ask ourselves how it impacts the people in our lives.

We saw earlier how people who grow up in an environment in which a parent is unable to regulate emotions in a healthy way can themselves develop a disregulated central nervous system and an inability to regulate emotions.

There is also a collective shadow that can be cast, the shadow of the collective emotional states in a house or office. This shadow is not necessarily created by one person but is a representation of all the emotional energies in that place. Once this collective emotional shadow is cast, everyone in that environment will be feeding off it, and depending on what this shadow is, it has the ability to help everyone or hurt everyone.

I have witnessed corporate organisations where the culture and shadows cast have had huge impacts on employees' health and well-being. Imagine a corporate organisation where management constantly pushes employees to work long hours, disregards personal boundaries and prioritises unrealistic deadlines over employee well-being. The environment becomes one of constant stress and pressure, with little regard for work–life balance.

Over time, this culture of intense work expectations and disregard for personal boundaries takes its toll on the employees. They begin to experience physical symptoms such as chronic stress, exhaustion and sleep disturbances. As the pressure continues, some employees develop health issues like frequent headaches, migraines and even digestive problems.

The destructive energy within the organisation not only affects physical health but also impacts work performance. The employees become burnt out and lose motivation, resulting in decreased productivity. The constant pressure to meet unreasonable goals leads to an increase in mistakes, missed deadlines and a decline in the quality of work.

Moreover, the negative culture leads to strained relationships between colleagues, as everyone is competing to meet the demanding expectations. This further deteriorates the overall work environment, hindering collaboration and creativity.

In this example, the destructive energy and culture within the organisation not only harms the employees' physical and mental health but also hinders their ability to perform their best work. It's a clear demonstration of how the shadows we cast can have a detrimental effect on both the individuals and the overall success of the organisation.

Children pick up on everything – not just what is said or what is done, but every emotion, every energy, every frequency in the home. When you look back at your home and the environment in which you grew up, what were the shadows that were cast? Who was casting them? What energy were those shadows filled with – was it joyful and full of fun or was it angry and full of fear?

The way we handle anger, the way we handle fear, the way we express our emotions sends ripple frequency waves through our house, through our workplace and within the environments where we find ourselves. One of the greatest pieces of work we can do is to explore and become curious about our own emotional shadows, to understand the way in which we emotionally express ourselves and to examine the suppressed emotions we unconsciously spread. Every one of us must be aware of the shadows in which we live or have lived and we must be aware of the shadows we cast.

Maybe there are only two human emotions, maybe even only one

When we talk about emotions and try to pinpoint what our own conscious or unconscious emotional state is, we often think of a whole spectrum of emotions: shame, guilt, anger, frustration, joy, gratitude, happiness, the list goes on and on.

However, I believe that when we really understand these emotions, we find that there are only two human emotions. I believe the heart of every emotion and the root cause of all emotion can be distilled down to two primary emotional states, and these can be identified as either love or fear. When we're in an emotional state of love, the emotion of love can manifest in many ways, such as joy, gratitude, patience, compassion and kindness. Many of the instances in this section spoke about how we react emotionally from a place of fear. When we are in the emotion of fear, it can manifest as impatience, anger, frustration, jealousy, comparison. But at the root of all these emotional descriptions or emotional extensions is either love or fear. We live in a world where we are bombarded constantly with fearful messages, highlighting the uncertainty and unpredictability of the world we live in and all the things we need to be afraid of. But this is a one-dimensional news agenda. We never hear about all the incredible things that are happening at every given second of every day, we don't see news reports about all the babies being born healthy every minute, or all the people falling in love or the moments of joy and happiness that people experience each day. News is not designed to set our soul alive with gratitude or joy or love: it is designed to terrify and threaten; and the problem with the one-dimensional, agenda-driven content is that it is endless, on every platform 24 hours a day. We live in a world where fear is now the driving emotion and where a new threat is being beamed into our homes, our minds and our hearts every single day. We live in a world where fear is the new normal.

We also live in a world where we are constantly being programmed to compare ourselves to others, to believe we are not good enough, a world where people are forever being criticised. We are all the time being measured, from our work performances, to the number of steps we take, to the hours we sleep, the calories we burn, and then it extends to how well we are doing as parents, with endless books and social media accounts telling us our babies should be sleeping all night, they should be asleep by 7 p.m., every single developmental milestone they should be hitting. And then endless sites telling us the life we should be living, the places we should be seeing ... And all of this is a constant, constructed effort to create a lack mindset where people are being bombarded with this fictitious version of reality that leaves them thinking their reality is somehow lacking – because they are not good enough, not good enough at work, not good enough in relationships, not good enough as mums, not good enough as dads, not fit enough, not happy enough, not rich enough. And all this feeds into a deep erosion of self-esteem, to the point where we begin to think that if our life is so lacking, it must be something lacking in us, something not good enough in us, and this creates shame and guilt, which are all symptoms of fear – fear that we are not good enough and that we are failing our children, our partners, and that we are failing in our lives.

The more I look at my own emotions, the more I reflect on the times where I've been impatient. The impatience was a symptom of my fear that I wasn't working quickly enough, and that led to a fear of missing an opportunity. My impatience was just a symptom of my fear.

When I look at the times when I have been angry, I have been angry at people for various reasons but when I break it all down I was angry at them because they were challenging me or my beliefs, which made me feel fearful that they didn't respect me – or even deeper, their actions were touching a raw emotional nerve inside of me that maybe I wasn't good enough and maybe they were right.

It's important that we begin to understand these two primary human emotions. These are powerful motivations that I believe are driving our unconscious emotional states, and thereby informing how we react emotionally to life happening around us. We can spend our life driven by fear, rushing, racing, anxiously chasing, striving, all in an attempt to get away from what we fear. Or we can shift our emotional responses and begin to live in a state of love, in openness and gratitude, in a state of abundance, focused and moving towards what we want and what we love. When we look at our own life, when we look at the way we live, the things we think about, the stories that

If we examine the emotions of love and fear and push it a little further, maybe there is only one human emotion – love.'

run through our mind, it's important to ask: Am I living my life from a place of fear or a place of love?

If we examine the emotions of love and fear and push it a little further, maybe there is only one human emotion – love – and maybe fear is simply the absence of love. What we need to understand is that fear and love cannot co-exist; we cannot be in a state of love and fear at the same time. Fear and love are different chemical and energy realities that use different systems in our bodies, and these cannot be switched on simultaneously. Our centres of survival require so much energy that when these systems are switched on and we are living in anxiety and fear, we are viewing the world from the perspective of threat. The brain then energises survival systems in the body which conclude that being happy or being grateful isn't as important as simply surviving, and so it switches off the heart centres of joy, love and gratitude.

As we now know, our brain is a powerful threat-detection system and it takes over in times of perceived threat or danger, and as long as our brain is getting all this energy, all our blood flow is going to our hindbrain, which is our survival mode. The hormones of stress take over our senses, so we focus on all possible threats and we create an echo chamber of terror and fear. When we move into a state of love or gratitude we are redirecting our energy, our awareness and our blood flow away from the hindbrain, away from our survival systems and towards our heart. When we ignite the frequency of the heart we begin to experience a new frequency, a new energy; our brain starts to release different chemicals such as oxytocin and we feel a physical and mental feeling of connection, of love and of gratitude. Now our brain and our body are responding to this new energy of possibility and creation and are no longer trapped in the energy of survival.

What if we have an inner emotional choice?

Without deeper questioning, it is easy to think that it's natural or normal to live in a fearful, stressful, uncertain, unpredictable emotional state because the outside world is in an uncertain and unpredictable state. But if we assume that our emotions are generated and maintained by the outside world alone, then we have just surrendered our emotional health and one of our greatest freedoms: our emotional freedom.

What if, on deeper and closer inspection, you were to find out that your inner emotional state is not actually generated or maintained by the outside world but by you and you alone? What if you began to realise that each and every one of us has a powerful choice and that one of the most powerful choices we have is our emotional choice.

What if you were to discover that even in this uncertain, unpredictable world, your inner world, your inner emotional state, your emotional health, can be predictable, can be sustainable, can be consistent and can be governed by you to be whatever you want it to be, regardless of the outside world?

Press Pause

Can you think of the last time you felt pure joy in your life?

On a scale of one to ten, how joyful would you say your life is right now?

What is depleting joy in your life?

What could you do to cultivate more joy in your life?

Can you, at times, take yourself and life too seriously?

Would you be willing to let your inner child out to play?

Before we go further: the physical dimension of emotions

The word 'emotion' has existed in English since the seventeenth century, originating as a translation of the French *émotion*, meaning a physical disturbance. An emotion is a chemical and electrical signal released by the brain and sent into the body as a strong feeling usually directed toward a specific object – an external reality or an internal creation of our mind – and is an adaptive response, part of the vital process of normal reasoning and decision-making. Emotions help us to act quickly in important situations. For example, when we're about to cross the street and see a car coming swiftly, the emotion of fear gives us a heightened focus and the physiological and mental energy to jump out of the way in a split second. Emotional experiences have three components: (a) a subjective experience (an emotion or feeling that is happening inside the person); (b) a physiological response (chemical and physical changes being made in the body); and (c) a behavioural or expressive response (how we act on or out of an emotion).

In a physiological sense, emotions arise from the activation of specialised groups of neurons in the brain. The emotional part of the brain is called the limbic brain, which is located underneath the cerebral cortex and just above the brainstem. The limbic system controls the experience and expression of emotions, as well as some automatic functions of the body. By producing emotions (such as fear), the limbic system enables people to behave in ways that help them communicate and survive physical and psychological upsets and threats. Fear is one of the most basic human emotions. It is programmed into the nervous system and works like an instinct. From the time we're infants, we are equipped with the survival instincts necessary to respond with fear when we sense danger or feel unsafe.

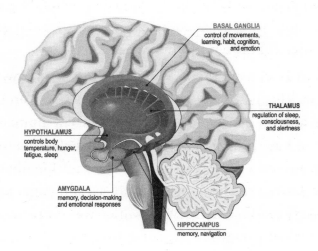

Emotions begin in our brain but quickly enter our body

Emotions are produced by the chemical and electrical signals sent into the body from the brain in response to an external or internal event. When the brain identifies a threat it quickly releases chemicals such as adrenaline and cortisol which evokes emotions such as fear or anxiety, and when it experiences something it thinks is safe or desirable it quickly releases dopamine and oxytocin which evokes emotions such as love and happiness.

Primal emotions such as love and fear emerge from the ancient limbic part of our brain, not from the newer, more advanced parts of the thinking brain. It is unclear whether there is a specific brain region for specific emotions – neuroscience is yet to show that – but what we do know is that the amygdala, which is part of the limbic brain, plays a massive role in the strength and the power of our emotions. Brain imagery can show the amygdala as it changes and grows depending on our emotional state. We know that the more active the amygdala is, the more powerful the emotion experienced.

Our brain is constantly looking for threats or rewards in the universe. This is necessary to keep us alive, safe and aware of danger, and was especially pertinent when humans first inhabited the Earth and it was populated by dangerous animals and numerous other threats. The brain traditionally placed more importance on emotions such as fear and anger as these were necessary for our very survival, which was more important than happiness, especially in those early days.

If a threat is detected, be it real, imaginary or even a memory, the brain doesn't distinguish between those things: instead it activates an emotional reaction. Simply thinking about something creates an emotional reaction which in turn triggers a chemical, physiological reaction. The moment a threat or reward is detected internally or externally, the feeling part of the brain alerts us to these through the release of chemical messages. Note that I am using the word 'reaction' here. The limbic brain is exceptionally fast at reacting but is less effective at responding, and as we learn more about emotional freedom, we will see the important difference between a reaction and a response.

The effect of emotional dis-health on the body

We can measure and observe the impact emotions have on our chemistry, our physiology and our nervous system, our immune system and our hormonal system.

Mind and body are an interconnected union that constantly interact with each other in a way that is inseparable, where changes in one lead to immediate and correlating changes in the other. Western science has endless scientific data to prove this interconnection between mind, emotions and physical expression, but western medicine has often wrongly downplayed it and as a result it can overly focus on treating the physical expression or the physical symptoms and never actually get to or treat the underlying emotional cause. When we don't treat the root cause, the physical symptoms might change but the emotional disease will keep finding a way into the body and we will keep getting physically sick. We need to think on a much wider scale; we need to think about our health and wellness in a way that reflects and honours this unity of systems.

What shows up in our emotions shows up in our immune and hormonal systems

Our nervous system is a giant electrical system. It connects all the systems in the body and all the organs in the body with the brain. We know that the emotional centres of the brain are connected to the nervous system, to the immune system and to the hormonal system, and we know that what happens in our emotions shows up in our nervous system, in our immune system and in our hormonal system. At all points, the brain, the immune system and the hormonal system are in constant chemical communication with each other, creating correlating chemistry. Negative emotions can reduce our immunity, whereas when we're in a more positive mindset our immunity is more robust.

We are chemically motivated by our brain, through the release of a powerful neurotransmitter called dopamine, to pursue anything we interpret as a reward, and we are chemically activated, through the release of adrenaline and cortisol, to run away from or fight anything that is interpreted as a threat. The production of these chemicals alerts us to what the brain deems as safe or unsafe and plays an important role in activating different systems.

Understanding our sympathetic and parasympathetic nervous systems

Two very different parts of our autonomic nervous system can be activated depending on what we are facing or even perceived to be facing. If our brain detects a threat, we experience an emotion such as fear which activates the sympathetic nervous system, a vital part of our make-up. Very often our sympathetic nervous system gets a bad name because of its link with stress and the fight-or-flight response. But since the beginning of time, this system and its fight-or-flight response was intended as a survival mechanism so that mammals, including humans, could react quickly to life-threatening situations. Using our sympathetic nervous system correctly and for short periods is very healthy, as it's an important mechanism by which we can avoid or overcome threats, and it gives us the extra alertness, energy and focus we need at times. However, staying in our sympathetic nervous system for sustained periods is not only unhealthy, but also has a massive negative impact on our happiness and our mental and physical well-being.

Once the sympathetic nervous system is activated through perceived threat, the brain releases stress hormones such as cortisol and adrenaline. Adrenaline increases our heart rate, elevates our blood pressure and boosts energy supplies. Cortisol, the primary stress hormone, increases sugars (glucose) in the bloodstream, enhances our brain's use of glucose and increases the availability of substances that repair tissues. When this happens we become agitated, we find it hard to concentrate or focus, we can start to sweat, we lose our appetite and we begin to catastrophise.

Cortisol and adrenaline are closely linked, and they play an intrinsic role in our overall health. Cortisol helps our body's use of fats, proteins and carbohydrates and helps to regulate our metabolism. However, prolonged elevation of these hormones can be damaging, and so managing stress and learning how to keep cortisol and adrenaline levels in balance is essential to maintaining a healthy quality of life. Common signs and symptoms of excess cortisol include weight gain (especially in the face and abdomen), fatty deposits between the shoulder blades, diabetes, hypertension, hirsutism in women, proximal muscle weakness and osteoporosis.

The other side of our autonomic nervous system is our parasympathetic nervous system (PSNS), a network of nerves that relaxes the body after periods of stress or danger. It is responsible for stimulation of rest-and-digest or feed-and-breed activities. It helps run life-sustaining processes such as digestion, sexual arousal, salivation, lacrimation (production of tears), urination and defecation. When the parasympathetic nervous system is activated, it slows our heart and breathing rates and can lower blood pressure. When our body enters a state of relaxation, this relaxation breeds recovery by switching back on our parasympathetic nervous system. The more time we spend in a PSNS state, the healthier we are.

Here is a very simple and practical example. Think of someone pulling a gun on you; think of that moment where you are staring down the barrel and imagine what would happen straight away in your inner world. Your immediate emotional reaction is fear and this sends chemical signals racing through your body. Your heart rate increases, your breathing instantly becomes fast and shallow, your brain releases cortisol and adrenaline and all your stress centres are immediately triggered. From a biological and chemical point of view, your body recognises the emotion of fear and this acute stress activates your sympathetic nervous system, switching on your fight-or-flight systems to give you a boost of energy, and in order to have the energy to power the sympathetic nervous system it has to turn off your parasympathetic nervous system, which in turn turns off your immune system. It has to turn off all the systems associated with rest-and-digest, because at that moment the most important thing is survival at all costs – not healing, not growing, not developing. It is a short-term, high-cost response to a high-risk situation. Once we experience a threat to our safety – be it real or imagined – the hormones and chemicals associated with survival take over. We switch off all our systems that are connected to health, healing and well-being within the parasympathetic system for that period of time.

Once the situation has ended and the emotion fades, you are no longer in danger. Your intelligent brain recognises that the immediate threat has disappeared and that you are now safe, and the stress response is switched off, your sympathetic nervous system is deactivated and your rest-and-recovery system, your parasympathetic nervous system, kicks back in. This changes your chemistry, your immune system switches back on and your cells and genes go back to thriving mode and no longer survival.

As you can now see, there are incredibly multidimensional systems at play within our bodies. While all of the multi-dimensional systems are switching on and off, most of us are unaware of them, which is all part of the incredible intelligence of the human mind and body. But unless we become aware of them, we may never get the opportunity to control and regulate them. So instead of these systems serving us and our life choices, we end up serving these systems, and thus our life choices are controlled by our reactions to these systems. Therefore learning to regulate is key to taking back control over our sense of inner ease and peace.

Press Pause

Can you think of a value or belief you hold about yourself? In your work, this could be your sense of professionalism or pride in your attention to detail. In your relationships, this could be that you see yourself as caring, open or empathetic. You might see yourself as a good mother, father or friend. What happens when someone says something that challenges this? How do you react? Do you immediately go from 0 to 60 in fight mode, determined to refute what has been said to you? Or do you shut down, distance yourself? This is your sympathetic nervous system reacting to prevent you from getting hurt, from disrupting your sense of self, even though the threat is simply emotional.

We can carry a fear of abandonment, a sense of having to earn love or a fear of being 'less than'. We can carry these unconscious emotions into every aspect of our lives and they inform all of our emotional reactions to real, imagined and emotional threats.

Life is not a marathon, it's a series of sprints with important recovery built in between them

There is an expression that says life is a marathon and not a sprint, and we should live our lives at a steady pace the way a marathon runner runs a race. But this doesn't really make sense when you look at these two incredible nervous systems. There is a reason why we have a sympathetic and a parasympathetic nervous system: we are meant to be challenged, we are meant to be exposed to danger and threat, and when we are, we grow, we adapt and we become stronger. Then we are meant to recover. Our life is not supposed to be like a marathon; it's more sprint, recover, sprint, recover, accessing and using both systems and spending the right amount of time in each. But in our modern world the importance of recovery is underplayed and we are spending far too long in the sympathetic sprint mode – we are trying to sprint and sprint and sprint again and this is where the greatest danger lies. The constant sprinting and never slowing down or switching off is causing a build-up of prolonged stress, also known as chronic stress. I believe the greatest threat to human health in our modern world is not acute stress, it's chronic stress.

Understanding our emotional default mode

The emotional responses or emotional default modes that most people are aware of are fight or flight, which I have mentioned earlier, but there are four main responses: fight, flight, freeze and flow.

Let's take a look at each.

Fight

The fight response is a response of the sympathetic nervous system. It is where we step into the threat, we step into the activity and we get busy doing things. The fight response refers to the old idea of having to fight a bear or other deadly animal. Early humans had to be always on the lookout for such threats and ready to fight or flee quickly when they appeared.

But of course in modern life we don't have to face many physical bears; the 'bears' we face can be financial worries, parenting, work stresses and all the different things that challenge us on a daily basis. The fight response involves a heightened focus and awareness and a heightened sense of wanting to meet the challenge immediately and head-on, which is usually helpful. An exaggerated or over-activated fight response brought on by the presence of threat, or even the thought of a threat, means that we are perpetually in a state of fight or force, constantly finding people to argue with and things to argue against. In this state, it can feel like the entire world is out to get us and life is one constant battle. When we get locked into this 'fight' emotional reaction it means we can often lack the perspective we need to create a new and healthier situation.

Flight

In the flight response we run from the challenge. Again, using the analogy of being confronted by the bear, we don't fight the bear – instead we quickly assess that the bear is too big, too strong and too dangerous and we turn and run. Very often in these situations flight is actually the correct response; it is an assessment of the size and scale of the danger and quickly identifying that the safest thing is to withdraw from that danger. Flight response does not mean that we are a coward or scared, and many times in the face of danger it is important that we take time to retreat, to think and reflect. But an exaggerated or over-activated flight response means that we are always retreating, always backing down, always conceding our boundaries and our dreams for fear of upsetting someone, of causing conflict or of hurting others.

Freeze

The freeze response is a parasympathetic response that happens when our sympathetic nervous system becomes so activated into a heightened state of alertness that the parasympathetic nervous system tries to compensate and rebalance it, and in doing so the parasympathetic nervous system overpowers the sympathetic nervous system and shuts it down. The freeze response shuts down our ability to fight or flee and it literally leaves us with a sense of playing dead. For many animals in the wild, playing dead is an extraordinarily clever way of utilising a defensive system, and humans actually have the same inbuilt ability. It takes our energy and alertness out of the sympathetic system to the point where we feel tired and lethargic and we can almost play dead. Again, this is not a negative response – at times this can be a very important mechanism that saves us from the over-activation and chemical abundance of the sympathetic nervous system, and used in short periods the freeze response can be a very powerful way of regulating our nervous system, our brain activity and our emotions until we have time and space to plan a response.

The freeze response can also happen when we are exposed

to highly significant emotions of stress, fear or trauma. When that level of stress or trauma is simply not possible for the brain to process, the conscious brain will store these emotions beyond conscious awareness until we have the time and resources to deal with them. This can be a very important and healthy functioning of the freeze response. However, just like the fight and flight responses, the freeze response in a short-term setting is powerful and helpful, but when it becomes our consistent and dominant way of functioning, it is far less healthy.

People who live long term in the freeze response begin to feel a sense of emotional disassociation, a sense of lethargic energy. They can also begin to experience lengthy periods where they simply can't take action – leading to procrastination in their life. Procrastination has nothing to do with being lazy, nothing to do with being a perfectionist. Procrastination is where we are caught in a freeze response. And we simply haven't the energy to drive the actions that we want to take.

Flow

The fourth response is a beautiful mix of sympathetic and parasympathetic nervous states where we experience the coherence between the brain, the gut and the heart.

In the flow state we are alert but at ease, engaged but relaxed. It is a beautiful balance between alertness and calmness. The flow state is a state of coherence where the prefrontal cortex of our brain is alert and awake, giving us increased awareness and logical reasoning. In this flow state, our breathing rate is regulating our nervous system and we have created a very important space between stimulus and response that means we are no longer operating from pre-conditioned emotional reflexes but from a place of conscious awareness. In a flow state we begin to achieve a sense of slowing down on the inside that appears to also slow down the outside world. We can begin to distort our perception of time and space and to see opportunities where others don't. The flow state is by far the most powerful force we can be in; it empowers our brain and our body to regulate our energy, our awareness and our attention into a place of control. This empowerment brings us into a state of coherence, and it is in this flow state where we can best deal with the uncertainty, adversity and opportunity of life.

It is important that we begin to identify within ourselves which of these responses is our immediate response mode. Do we rise and meet the challenge head-on, with anger, aggression and force, or do we turn and run? Do we like to have or need the time and space to stop, think, reflect and to get away from the source of apprehension? Having conscious awareness of our response and knowing when to stay there and when to leave is important for our overall health, vitality and healing.

Acute and chronic stress and acute and chronic emotional distress

The body's stress response system is usually self-limiting, and once a perceived threat has passed, hormone levels return to normal as adrenaline and cortisol levels drop, our heart rate and blood pressure return to baseline levels, and other systems resume their regular activities. The brain and the body find it hard to distinguish between fear, fatigue and over-activation, and in many ways all three result in the same unhealthy loading on our inner systems. In our modern world we are always rushing and racing, always looking down the barrel of an imaginary gun. The danger of living in this always-on mode is stress, whether acute or chronic.

Acute stress is short-lived, whereas chronic stress is a consistent build-up of stress over an extended period. This stress may not be coming from one particular source but may be made up of lots of little stresses coming from a number of different areas such as work, relationships, children, finances and so on. And while bursts of acute stress are actually good for us, chronic stress is the opposite: it leads to chronic illness.

The scenario we used earlier of someone pointing a gun at us is an obvious example of high stress in what we call an acute stress situation, and this type of acute stress is exactly what the sympathetic nervous system is designed for – a short, high-intensity burst that we experience rarely in exceptional circumstances – and when used in this way the sympathetic nervous system is highly effective and adds to our growth and our health and wellness. But in today's world, with constant negative news, we are living in a prolonged state of fear: fear for our children, the planet, our job security, our safety. Emotions like fear, shame, anger and blame release stress chemicals such as adrenaline and cortisol, which can become addictive, so addictive in fact that when we don't have them we start to crave them. This often leads to a self-perpetuating cycle of addiction and destructive emotions, which causes chronic emotional stress.

This prolonged chronic emotional distress leads to our emotions going unregulated, meaning that this cascade of hormones, neurotransmitters and nerve chemicals has a profound effect on our adrenal glands and can cause adrenal fatigue, also affecting the cells of the immune system. This puts us at increased risk of many conditions, including anxiety, depression, digestive issues, headaches, muscle tension and pain, heart disease, heart attack, high blood pressure, stroke, sleep problems, weight gain and concentration impairment. Emotional fatigue and emotional burnout are now a common part of our modern world and they are having a massive negative impact on our physical health, which in turn impacts our spiritual space and our mental mood.

Adrenal glands and adrenal burnout

The term 'adrenal fatigue' has been used to explain a group of symptoms that occur in people who are under long-term mental, emotional or physical stress. If we are constantly living in the emotions of chronic stress, if we are constantly living in a sympathetic dominant state, then this heightened emotional state can lead us to adrenal fatigue.

Our adrenal glands are endocrine glands and are located on top of our kidneys. They are controlled in part by our hypothalamus and pituitary gland. The hypothalamus is a small area of the brain involved in hormonal regulation.

Our adrenal glands consist of two main parts:

- Medulla: The medulla is the inner part of the adrenal gland, and it releases the hormones adrenaline (epinephrine) and noradrenaline (norepinephrine). These hormones help control our blood pressure, heart rate, sweating and other activities that are also regulated by our sympathetic nervous system.
- Cortex: The cortex is the outer part of the adrenal gland, and it releases corticosteroid and mineralocorticoid hormones. The adrenal cortex also stimulates the production of small amounts of male sex steroid hormones (androgenic steroids).

As mentioned above, the adrenal glands produce many important hormones, including cortisol, aldosterone and adrenaline. These adrenal hormones help regulate several bodily functions including metabolism, blood pressure and the body's response to stress.

- Cortisol is a glucocorticoid hormone that plays several important roles. It helps control the body's use of fats, proteins and carbohydrates. It also suppresses inflammation and regulates blood pressure, increases blood sugar and helps control our sleep–wake cycle. Our adrenal glands release cortisol during times of stress to help our body get an energy boost and better handle an emergency.

- Aldosterone is a mineralocorticoid hormone that plays a central role in regulating blood pressure and the levels of sodium and potassium (electrolytes) in the blood. This means aldosterone helps regulate our blood pH (how acidic or basic it is) by controlling the electrolyte levels.
- Adrenaline and noradrenaline, the fight-or-flight hormones, are known as catecholamines. They are capable of raising our heart contractions, increasing blood flow to the muscles and brain and assisting in glucose metabolism. They also control the squeezing of our blood vessels (vasoconstriction), which helps maintain blood pressure. Our adrenal glands often release these hormones, and other adrenal hormones, when we are in physically and emotionally stressful situations.

All of these hormones are important, and in the right amounts add to our ability to live, adapt, evolve and survive. The danger is when we begin to experience them in high quantities and over prolonged periods, at which point they can become destructive to our health and happiness.

Gut–brain connection and the microbiome

For too long we thought of the gut only as an organ of digestion. Of course, it is a very important organ of digestion, but it is so much more than that. The gut is an immune organ, which has an incredible ability to keep us healthy and to fight against illnesses and bacteria; in fact it is our greatest ally in fighting disease. But the gut is also a sensory organ that is constantly taking in data from our brain, our heart, our chemistry and our external environment. The gut, which is now known as the second brain, is constantly communicating with the brain. In fact, five times more communication is transferred from the gut to the brain than from the brain to the gut. Therefore the emotions we experience play a huge role in the health of our gut and the health of our microbiome.

The microbiome refers to the collection of microbes that live in our body, such as bacteria, fungi and viruses, and their genes that naturally live on our bodies and inside us. Although these microbes are so small they require a microscope to be seen, they contribute in very important ways to our health and wellness. Our gut microbiome is made up of trillions of bacteria, fungi and other microbes and plays a key role in maintaining good health by helping to control digestion and benefiting our immune system.

The links between emotional regulation and the gut microbiome demonstrate how physical health influences emotions and vice versa. Stress can lead to changes in both the numbers (abundance) and types (diversity) of bacteria. This can have an impact on our ability to regulate our mood via the gut–brain communication system known as the hypothalamic-pituitary-adrenal (HPA) axis. Research suggests that the gut microbiome is responsible for communicating with the nervous system and immune system, affecting overall mood. Many people think of depression and anxiety as a chemical imbalance in the brain. But these chemicals are created in the gut, not the brain. In fact, more than 30 different neurotransmitters and nearly

90 per cent of the body's serotonin, the feel-good hormone, come from our gut.

The gastrointestinal tract is sensitive to emotion, anger, anxiety, sadness, elation – all of these emotions (and others) can trigger symptoms in the gut. Just as the food we eat has a direct impact on our brain, the brain has a direct effect on the stomach and intestines. Studies have found that people who suppress their emotions have a less diverse gut microbiome. Stress can drive and augment numerous gastrointestinal issues, including irritable bowel syndrome and multiple inflammatory bowel diseases. Chronic stress is associated with reduced diversity in the microbiome and increased intestinal permeability. Research suggests that stress not only alters intestinal mucosa permeability and cytokine secretion (small proteins that are crucial in controlling the growth and activation of immune cells) but also may significantly change the community structure and activity of the commensal microbiota in the gut. In turn, gut microbiota may influence stress-related physiological responses.

We must now begin to think of the entire body as one unified, connected system. What shows up in our emotions shows up in our immune system, in our nervous system and in our hormonal systems.

Now that we have explored the impact that our emotions can have on our physical health, I hope it helps to sharpen our focus on the importance of emotions and the importance of developing the ability to regulate our emotions. Far too many times I meet people who allow unhelpful and destructive emotions to exist because they don't realise the impact those emotions are having on their health, and far too often I see people who seem to think that emotions can be ignored and that we just get through them or simply wait for them to pass, as though they don't make a difference or we don't have a choice. But our health is far too important, our happiness is far too important and therefore our emotional health is far too important to ignore these things.

Now that we have examined how emotional dis-health can affect our behaviour and our physical bodies, we can look at the steps we can take to begin living with good emotional health and equilibrium. In the section 'The Emotional Choice', we will look closely into how we can practically do the work of addressing all these conscious and unconscious emotions. But before this, there is another step, 'The Awareness Shift'. Only by becoming aware of our emotional state and the situations and events that caused them can we begin to change and dissolve them with clarity and certainty. In the following section, we will explore how we can achieve a greater level of awareness and insight into ourselves and how we can begin to observe ourselves and the things that have happened to us without judgement or fear. We will explore the powerful reality of the observer self and how we can literally begin to see ourselves and our lives as if we are having an out-of-body experience. When we awaken the observer self we begin to transcend the noise of the physical body, the chemical and physiological noise, and we literally begin to see ourselves from outside our physical reality. We will also explore why many of us find it difficult to access or stay in the state of the observer self and we will meet the enemy of the observer self, the ego. It's time to examine awareness.

Press Pause

The 4-7-8 breathing technique introduced by Dr Andrew Weil, an American doctor and thought leader in the field of integrated medicine, is a wonderful practice that enables your body to drop into the parasympathetic nervous system. This will help reduce the amount of stress you feel in your body and mind and will also aid the body in its healing and restorative processes for enhanced health and vitality.

- *To begin, make sure you're comfortable, in a seated position. Place the tip of your tongue to the roof of your mouth, just behind your front teeth.*
- *Begin by taking a slow, deep breath in through the nose for the count of four. Send this breath down to your belly and let it rise. Imagine your belly blowing up like a balloon – very gently and soft.*
- *At the top of this breath, pause for a count of seven.*
- *Then slowly exhale through your mouth, pursing your lips and making a 'whoosh' sound for a count of eight.*
- *Repeat the cycle up to four times.*
- *This breathing pattern aims to reduce stress and anxiety and create more inner calm.*

SUMMARY

- What is emotional health?
- How good is your emotional health?
- Emotions are not positive or negative
- Where we project our emotions is seldom the root cause of the emotion
- The effect of expressing our emotions
- Our negative emotional bias
- What happens when we meet our emotional pain (are we embarrassed by our emotions and to show them?)
- What the mind supresses, the body expresses
- Our addiction to stress chemicals and why we keep on poking the bear
- Experiencing negative emotions in the absence of a real threat
- How we store emotions: our conscious (temporary) emotions and our unconscious emotions and the effect of both
- How our emotional states are affected by the absence of primary emotional needs and the presence of trauma and beliefs
- Understanding our beliefs and where they come from better: the influence of family dynamics
- Maybe there are only two emotions? Maybe only one?
- What if we had emotional choice?

How emotions show up in the body
- Their effect on our immune and hormonal systems and our sympathetic and parasympathetic nervous systems
- Understanding our emotional default mode
- The effect of acute and chronic stress and acute and chronic emotional distress
- Adrenal glands and adrenal burnout
- Gut–brain connection and the microbiome

2

The Awareness Shift

Consciously changing our emotional states

We have just examined emotions – where they come from, the fact that they can be powerful messengers or destructive inhibitors that can negatively impact our ability to enjoy life and to be at peace with life, and how they can also have a massive impact on our physical health if they are unmanaged. With this new focus we now look at how we can manage our emotions in a more proactive and healthy way. We need to learn how to become the conscious observer and regulator of our emotions.

While emotions like joy, love and gratitude can be extraordinary, being in a constant emotional state is not always necessary. We may think that the absence of a positive emotion means the presence of negative emotion. But we need to rethink this. Do we always need to be chasing happiness or is it just

'Do we always need to be chasing happiness or is it just another temporary emotion that we can spend our life pursuing?'

another temporary emotion that we can spend our life pursuing? Maybe there is something beyond happiness, something beyond a state of emotion? What if there was an eternal state that isn't an emotion, that is simply a state of peace? Maybe peace is actually the ultimate state and, if so, where would this peace exist? Where in our human existence is there a place that is above temporary emotion, a place of ever-present awareness and peace that is free from our past situations, free from our memories, free from the challenges of the outside physical world? What if we had an infinite inner reservoir of peace? Would you like to find it?

The freedom choice

In life we can't always control what happens to us; life is uncertain and unpredictable by its very nature and we certainly can't control the universe. Viktor Frankl in his ground-breaking book *Man's Search for Meaning* illustrates that, while we can't always control what happens to us in life, we can always control our response.

Some of us will experience extreme pain through physical or psychological trauma, bereavement, loss and grief and each individual's experience of this is unique. But when it comes to the day-to-day challenges that life throws at us, the emotional wounds we carry, I believe that it's possible to move away from suffering. There is a difference between pain and suffering. Very often our suffering is caused by our internal emotional reaction to the pain and very often our suffering is deepened and perpetuated by something inside ourselves. Life does not have to get easier, it does not have to be without challenge or without pain, but we can get stronger and we can become emotionally free and when we do we take away our suffering. Something incredible happens when we make peace more powerful than pain and when we are more committed to peace than we are to our past or our pain – when we attach our energy and attention to our place of power and no longer our place of pain.

One of the most important aspects of living with this incredible freedom is discovering and activating our emotional choice. Once we become aware of our inner emotions and aware of where we are placing our attention and awareness, we can create a space between the stimulus and our response. If we are simply reacting immediately to external stimuli then we are like conditioned reflexes, constantly emotionally reacting to the external world with little conscious control or predictability. Without a higher awareness we can be held as emotional hostages of our past, of our beliefs about the outside world; we can be prisoners of our childhood. Once we achieve a higher level of awareness, we can move beyond un-conscious emotional reaction to a place of conscious response. It's important that we understand the difference between a reaction and a response: a reaction is an

> 'Life does not have to get easier, it does not have to be without challenge or without pain, but we can get stronger and we can become emotionally free.'

> 'It's important that we understand the difference between a reaction and a response: a reaction is an immediate instinct; a response is a conscious and deliberate choice.'

immediate instinct; a response is a conscious and deliberate choice.

External events are simply things that happen, but when we can control the meaning and interpretation we give them we can begin to reshape them, reframe them and place them into a new context which changes our emotional response.

Higher awareness allows us to move from emotional reactions to emotional responses

As just mentioned, an emotional reaction is an instant, unconscious, conditioned response that has little or no conscious thought. It's a learned reflex that is conditioned by our past and our unconscious emotional states, our fears, our deepest beliefs about the world and about ourselves. We have seen in the previous section that our emotional reactions and temporary emotions are formed through the lens of our unconscious emotional state which we have carried with us from childhood, along with our beliefs and values, and very often our emotional reaction to something is more to do with our memories and experiences than the situation itself. With a higher level of awareness we can begin to see the habits and patterns in our emotional reactions and can look with greater insight into the root cause of those reactions, and by doing so we get the chance to dissolve this root cause. And when we do, we untether the emotional ropes tying us to the past, which gives us the opportunity to create a new response.

Our immediate emotional *reaction* doesn't take time to reflect on what's actually happening, the unconscious emotion that is being triggered or what the best response might be. A reaction quickly rushes to a conclusion about the situation based on a memory, a belief or an expectation which may not be true. Such a reaction can actually be hurtful to ourselves, to our dreams, to our loved ones and to the wider community. I bet many of us have banged our leg off the corner of a chair or something in the house and often our immediate reaction is to kick back at it, or we have received a hurtful message and our immediate reaction is to reply with a similarly hurtful one; both of these reactions actually just prolong our agony or add to it, and the reason is our natural instinct is to hit back at the source of our pain.

A *response*, on the other hand, is a conscious decision we make after taking time to process the situation on its own merits and to ask some very important questions:

- What is the emotion that is being triggered in me right now?
- What is the belief that is creating that emotion?
- What would love do?

Awakening our higher awareness

Let's begin our exploration of this higher sense of awareness, this part of us that has the ability to exist above our temporary situations and above our emotions. If the brain is a threat-detection system, then if we remain within the world of the thinking brain we will also remain in a world of temporary emotional reactions and we will stay committed to surviving in a threat-filled world. There is a part of us that belongs to our physical identity and is constantly thinking and commenting on ourselves and our world and reacts to every experience through inner narratives, beliefs and emotions. This part is what we call 'the thinking self'. The thinking self is a lower consciousness, and while it can be extremely useful in navigating everyday situations quickly, we often have to move above this thinking brain because there are times where a quick reaction is not the best reaction.

In order to get to a higher sense of awareness, we need to move beyond our limbic brain, into our most powerful state of existence where our deepest peace resides. And to do this we must look at the duality of our existence.

The duality of our existence

There is a part of us that can move beyond this thinking self and local identity and instead peacefully notice and observe our thoughts and feelings. This self does not need to react to every situation and event because it is looking at our life not in the granular, micro moments of the everyday but in the greater expansiveness of existence. This self, which exists in our higher awareness, is called 'the observer self'.

'There is a part of us that can move beyond this thinking self and local identity and instead peacefully notice and observe our thoughts and feelings.'

While the thinking self can be found within the physical thinking brain, the part of our brain that is committed to fighting threat, the observer self is found in our higher awareness, our higher consciousness that is above the temporary and above the situation. And when we are in this level of awareness we are the one observing the experience and not just the one having the experience. It's like we can be both the chess piece and the chess player simultaneously. We can be having the experience while at the same time our higher awareness, our higher consciousness, allows us to see the experience in greater perspective.

When we awaken our observer state, when we enter this level of higher consciousness, we are accessing a field of connected consciousness, that is above an individual identity or a local field of awareness. So in my own case, when I observe the physical Gerry, the Gerry that is having an experience, that field of awareness from which I am observing Gerry is not actually Gerry, I have not created that field of awareness and I don't own it, it is simply awareness. This non-identity of the observer self is something that we can struggle with because we are so used to having labels for everything.

Lessons from spiritual traditions

The Christian tradition says that Jesus was both human and divine at the same time, both finite and infinite. Jesus was a man, he was the son of Mary and Joseph, he was at times scared, uncertain and vulnerable, and at the same time he always had the awareness that he was more than that, he was aware that he was connected to something more than his physical self and he knew that when he connected to this infinite part of himself he felt different: his fear disappeared, his anger dissipated, his resistance dissolved and all that was left was an overwhelming sense of love and forgiveness and a powerful sense of perspective. This duality of existence allowed him to function every day as a human, having a deeply human experience, immersed in all human emotions and thoughts, yet at all times he was able to navigate his way around his human limitations and fears because he connected to and was in conversation with this higher self that was above his human experience.

The Christian tradition tells us that this deeper sense of awareness, this deeper field of consciousness, is God. But what if we change the labels a little? What if we change the name God to awareness, pure awareness or pure consciousness.

What if we simply said Jesus had a direct line to a deeper sense of infinite awareness, and that we all possess the ability to access that? We are all, at all times, our finite, time-bound human self and at all times we are our infinite, timeless energy self, and it is in this energy self, in this field of awareness, that we receive our deepest and greatest intelligence, information and vision of reality.

We all have the ability to get to a place of emotional ease by accessing our observer self, but getting to this place isn't always easy. There is one major force inside us that doesn't want us to get to that level of freedom because it thinks if we do, we will not survive. As crazy as it sounds, there is a piece of ourselves keeping us away from peace. It's time to meet that piece of ourselves, our human ego.

The thinking self

The thinking self, located in the thinking brain, provides a running commentary, often fearful and judgemental, that can be full of comparison, assumption and resistance. This commentary is happening in relation to every event and every person in our life because the thinking self is constantly trying to understand life situations in order to create a vision of the world that it can predict and control and thus to keep us safe. With survival as its priority, the thinking self's stream of thoughts and images is mainly fear-based and constantly disrupts us from the ability to simply experience the moment without judgement.

This constant disruption, this constant inner commentary, can greatly decrease our quality of life and fill our precious moments with narratives and fears that often have very little grounding in reality. It's as though we are at the most beautiful orchestral recital in the world, but instead of being able to hear it, we have a constant disruptive soundtrack of fear playing in our headphones, drowning out the beautiful music. The universe, the present moment, is the orchestra and very often we're unable to experience it as it is because of the deafening commentary going on in our head.

Working from a place of unmet emotional needs and beliefs, the thinking self can generate an inner narrative where we tell ourselves 'I'm not good enough', 'I'm not smart enough', 'I don't have enough', 'I'm not seen enough'. If we repeat that message to ourselves often enough, then every external situation will be quickly manipulated to fit this inner narrative and we will be left with the emotions of guilt, fear and shame. With an overactive, threat-focused thinking self the world now becomes a terrifying place and we lose sight of the many miracles and the magic we could be witnessing; we become emotionally connected to everything that is wrong and we lose sight of everything else.

In order to have the strength it needs, the thinking brain brings in reinforcements; it brings in an army general to uphold its beliefs and its rules and this committed army general will fight anything and everyone in order to achieve control and obedience. It will fight other people, it will fight the outside world, it will fight the future and it will especially fight our observer self; it makes it its mission to drown our observer self and in doing so it takes over, takes control. Who is this army general in our thinking brain? It's our ego, an incredible, powerful and dedicated entity that we must get to know, understand and regulate if we are to access our higher awareness and the emotional freedom of the observer self.

Getting to know our ego

In *Awaken Your Power Within*, I introduced the concept of the human ego and showed how most of us have a misplaced understanding of what ego is and how it shows up in our lives. I explained that most people think that ego is something to do with a person who believes they are above or better than everyone else. Ego is often associated with the brash and self-absorbed, but this is not ego at all; this is simply self-centredness and obnoxiousness. Ego can be in full flight in the quietest, most reserved person you know.

Ego is the part of us that is linked to our feelings of safety and security, the part of us that clings to our past, our past experiences, our memories, our traumas and our beliefs. It combines all these things to give us a label for us to identify with. I am the quiet one, the one with no confidence, the one who never gets a break, the unlucky one – these are all labels we give ourselves, labels created by our ego to give us a distinct identity that is different to everyone else. The ego does not believe in connection but isolation and separation, and it needs to separate us in order to label who we are and who we are not.

The ego is always consciously or subconsciously committed to supporting the thinking brain – to keep us alive, keep us protected and away from danger, real, remembered or imagined. In order to do this, our ego is always in a state of high alert and it often keeps us locked into a state of anxiety, worry and fear. It is a construction of our thinking self: the consciousness that exists within the limits of the brain, designed to keep us alive.

We all have an ego. What differs between people is not the presence or the potential presence of ego but the nature and size of the ego and the work needed to regulate it. Our ego is not a bad part of us, it is not deliberately trying to derail us and our dreams, it is simply scared that we won't achieve them. The ego uses self-sabotage as a self-preservation tool; it is afraid that if we try something new, if we dare to go after our dreams and we fail, we will be devastated, and the ego doesn't want us to be devastated. The ego will gladly accept current unhappiness (the familiar and safe) rather than risking potential greater unhappiness if we take risks.

Only the observer self has the ability to witness this, to speak to our ego, to reassure it and to move beyond the fear.

The angry ego fears abandonment more than anything. Ego is the part of us that is always afraid that we are not enough, that we will be left behind and abandoned again. This going back to when, as early humans, being excluded by our tribe meant certain death. If we have had an experience of being abandoned in the past, our ego can store this memory and keep it as an active reality, which means we are always afraid of being abandoned. It can make it difficult for us to have deep, meaningful relationships, relationships where we dare to give our heart and soul and relationships of deep commitment. The fearful ego is so afraid you might be abandoned again that it will either find ways to prevent you getting into these relationships or it will find ways to sabotage them and get you out of them before you get hurt. The ironic thing is that all these actions to prevent us from feeling abandoned actually result in us being alone, and they further reinforce our deepest fear and belief that we will be abandoned and left behind. With the best will in the world our ego has an incredible way of creating the exact situations it fears.

The ego needs us to have possessions in order to have value. It is always afraid that without possessions to give us meaning and identity, we are worthless. An ego that doesn't believe in our true identity clings to anything and everything in the physical world to try to make sure

> 'Ego is the part of us that is always afraid that we are not enough, that we will be left behind and abandoned.'

that people see us as a success or that we have meaning. In this way the ego connects our self-worth to our job, our house, our car, to the things people say about us or the things we think people think about us.

The human ego is committed to one job, and that is to keep us alive, and the way it does that is by keeping us committed to living in the predictable future based on the remembered past, keeping us locked in familiar thinking patterns, in similar emotional responses and feelings, and in a one-dimensional vision of who we are. And it will fight anyone and anything that challenges this one-dimensional vision of who we are and will make sure that our future self will be an extension of our past self and that we will continue to think and feel in the future as we have in the past. The ego will trap us in untrue stories about who we are, what we can do and what we can achieve in order to prevent us from changing. It will very quickly dismiss anything or anyone that challenges it or risks it being exposed. If we encounter someone or something that has a different life vision, a different belief system or a different life choice, the ego will try to convince us that they are wrong.

The ego will do the same when we start to express ourselves differently. The moment we think *Maybe I could get the job*; *Maybe I could write a book*; *Maybe I could find true love*, the ego will quickly come in and dismiss the thought because the ego only knows us as the person we are now and the person we have always been – and that person doesn't have their dream job, has never written a book and has never found love.

The change-averse ego

> 'The "familiar past" is where the ego thrives, and it will do everything in its power to lock us into old stories and old beliefs.'

The ego confuses change with danger, confuses the unfamiliar with danger; it isn't committed to excellence or even happiness: it is only committed to short-term survival and keeping us trapped in the feelings and emotions of short-term survival. Our ego likes order and structure; it needs to see the world as black and white, where in order for me to be right you must be wrong, in order for me to win you must lose. The ego cannot deal with the complexity of life and its various dynamics and nuances. The 'familiar past' is where the ego thrives, and it will do everything in its power to lock us into old stories and old beliefs. To change anything about ourselves, to begin to see and speak about ourselves in a new way, to create new habits and routines, we first have to challenge and overcome our terrified ego that wants to trap us in the familiar, being the same old person having the same old experiences.

The ego needs to fight: it needs something to attack and defend

The ego can also be the manifestation of a frustrated, frightened spirit. It thrives on attack and competition, and an over-ignited ego finds compromise and surrendering very difficult, even if this is surrendering to love, to the needs of a loved one, to putting the needs of another ahead of our own and especially to accepting and believing that we are at our best and most alive when we are no longer focused on the service of self but in the connection to and service of something bigger than ourselves. The ego thrives on being seen and heard; it needs to be constantly validated and requires constant energy and attention. If the ego doesn't receive the validation it craves, we become depressed, angry or emotionally deprived, afraid that without the ego getting constant energy and attention it might die, and that if it does we will not survive without it.

Ego sees the universe as a problem to be solved and controlled and a threat to be defended against, whereas the observer sees the universe as a mystery to be enjoyed. The ego is always looking for the source of our pain and anger but the problem is that it is always looking outside and will not accept that, in fact, the ego itself is the source. It will manipulate our interpretation and experience of the outside world and will create inner stories to try to convince us that the source of all our pain and the source of all our fear is external – is someone or something out there – when in fact if we were to allow the observer self to speak it would tell us that the source of our pain and our fear is inside us, inside the prison of the angry, fearful ego.

The judgemental, defensive ego

Ego gives immediate judgements and labels to every situation and to every person we encounter without ever actually analysing, reflecting on or being patient enough to see how these things actually play out in the bigger picture. The ego is terrified that without all these labels to cling to, we will have no identity at all.

The ego is always ready to fight anything or anyone that challenges its deepest beliefs about who we are and about the universe; it is always ready to dismiss or discredit any behaviours that are different to our normal ones and will provide incredible stories as to why these potential new behaviours are wrong and why making this potential change to our life is wrong, or at least the wrong time. The ego will even fight ourselves the moment we begin to change for the better. If our past is full of sadness, disappointment and feelings of not being enough, these will be familiar to the ego which, committed to familiarity, will become addicted to these feelings and will fight anything that will change or has the potential to change them.

From my years of study, life experience and work with clients I have learned that dissolving the ego, quietening its voice and reducing the role it plays in our lives, our decisions and our happiness, is one of the most important things we can do; it is the starting point to engaging fully in our observing self and our path to emotional freedom.

'An unhealthy, over-activated ego shuts the gateway to pure consciousness and higher awareness and in doing so disconnects us from the truest and most powerful form of our existence.'

An unhealthy, over-activated ego shuts the gateway to pure consciousness and higher awareness and in doing so disconnects us from the truest and most powerful form of our existence. An unregulated ego becomes so scared of the vastness of the universe it will try to convince us that nothing else exists other than the stories, beliefs and vision of reality that exist within the ego. The ego is terrified that it can't protect us should we go outside of its limits. It acts like a concerned parent, so afraid their child will get hurt or injured or upset if it goes outside that they never allow the child out of the house. In some ways that child will be protected and in so many ways it will be robbed of incredible life experiences and personal growth opportunities.

The separation from our higher awareness brought about by the human ego creates a reality where we think that our local consciousness is the origin, the centre and the summit of all consciousness and that no other level of consciousness exists outside it. When this happens, we lose perspective, we lose a sense of who we really are, and we lose connection to our true being and to all things; we lose connection to our greater awareness and we lose connection to our observer self.

For as long as humans have existed we have had a tendency to become consumed with owning and possessing, with clinging to power. But in order for us to really experience who we truly are and the incredible level of awareness we all possess, we must develop a way of becoming less attached to the physical, temporary things; we must become less the one who is trying to own the experience and more the one who is peacefully observing the experience; we must become less the one resisting and judging what is happening and more the one who allows life to unfold as it needs while at all times placing our energy and attention in the places that give us power and autonomy and not pain and victimhood.

By awakening our observer self we see the universe for what it is – an expansive, powerful field of awareness that has an incredible inner intelligence that connects everything that is, and in this unfolding mystery we are here to witness, to observe, to grow, while at all times knowing that we are beings who have the ability to exist in the physical world while always remaining an energy being with an awareness that goes beyond anything physical. We are awareness having a physical experience.

Emotional loneliness

When the voice of the human ego is allowed to become too dominant in our mind it conjures up fear, self-doubt and a sense of isolation or disconnection. In order for us to exist with a deeper sense of connection, we must not allow the ego to create this sense of separation.

The human ego is terrified that if we're not defined by our physical being, by something tangible – a job title, a history, an experience – if we don't have physical, tangible evidence to prove who we are, then perhaps we don't exist. Very often we think that in order for our life to have purpose and meaning, in order for us to justify our existence, we need to be busy, we need to be doing things. We need these labels in order to justify our being and our sense of self-worth.

- What if I'm not my experience?
- What if I'm not my past?
- What if I'm not the job that I do?
- What if I'm not the things that I think I am?

When we strip away the labels and the roles we play in life, strip it all back, the question appears: who am I?

We spend so much of our time doing and trying to 'become', trying to become somebody, trying to achieve something. The deeper question is what are we actually searching for?

Very often, what we're actually searching for is a deeper feeling of connection, of being enough and of understanding who we are.

Feeding the ego, starving the soul

The ego needs constant energy and attention and as we give all our energy and resources to serving the ego, we are at the same time starving the soul. Removing self-limiting fear, releasing the ego-constructed paradigms and self-limiting beliefs allows us to remove all that separates us from our true identity, our true source. It is only when we arrive 'home' to our true source, 'home' to ourselves and our true identity that we can come to know inner peace. If we could only realise the incredible and connected source of power and peace that each and every one of us comes from and that our identity is so powerful that only our hearts can experience it. Connecting to our own deepest self, connecting to our deepest heart's truth is where we connect to and meet the universe, the divine.

Dissolving the human ego

Dissolving the human ego is a complex and ongoing process that requires self-awareness, reflection and dedicated effort. Here are some steps you can take towards dissolving the ego:

1. Cultivate self-awareness: Begin by observing your thoughts, emotions and reactions without judgement. The next time you are in a situation of high emotional stress, try to take a pause. If you're unable to do this while in the situation, try to do it directly or soon after. Ask yourself what part of your reaction in that situation came from your ego. Recognise when the ego is present and observe how it influences your actions and interactions with others.

2. Question your attachments: The ego often feeds off attachments to concepts, possessions, relationships and identities. Examine your attachments and question their importance and necessity. Challenge the idea that you are defined by these attachments.

3. Practise mindfulness and meditation: Engaging in regular mindfulness and meditation practices can enhance your ability to observe your thoughts and emotions without getting caught up in them. This allows you to create space between your true self and the ego.

4. Embrace vulnerability and humility: The ego often thrives on feelings of superiority, control and invulnerability. Embrace vulnerability and humility, allowing yourself to acknowledge and learn from your mistakes and limitations. Embracing imperfection and recognising that everyone has their own struggles can help dissolve the ego's need for superiority.

5. Cultivate empathy and compassion: Practise seeing situations from other people's perspectives and develop

empathy for their experiences. Cultivating compassion towards others helps break down the barriers created by the ego's need for self-centredness.

6.   Let go of the need for approval: The ego often seeks validation and approval from others. Learn to let go of the need for external validation and focus on self-acceptance and inner growth instead.

7.   Embrace interconnectedness: Recognise that you are a part of something much larger than yourself and that everything and everyone is interconnected. Develop a sense of unity and connectedness with others, nature and the world around you.

8.   Journaling: Put pen to paper to reflect on your actions. Journaling gives you a direct internal access to your sub-conscious mind and to the inner narratives you are holding.

Remember, dissolving the ego is a lifelong journey, and it's natural for the ego to resurface from time to time. Be patient and compassionate with yourself throughout this process.

While an unregulated ego can be our enemy, we can see that the thinking self, or the ego, is also a gateway through which the greater awareness of pure consciousness arrives, is processed and is understood in human terms. It is this awareness within the thinking self that allows us to experience the power and magnitude of the field of pure consciousness, without being overwhelmed by the vastness of the universe and the vastness of existence and consciousness. The ego is like an electrical regulator that can receive mains electricity and cut that power down so that our laptop gets only the voltage it needs. The ego is what we call the local field of awareness or consciousness through which we come to experience the world. Everyone has an ego and if regulated, if worked on and nurtured, it can be a beautiful friend.

Beyond ego

When we learn how to manage the ego, we can then let go of the need to control ourselves, those around us and/or our environment, and the need to understand and predict. By dissolving the edges of the ego, we can begin to live comfortably in the space between the no longer and the not yet. Without the loud and often angry voice of the ego we begin to experience another voice – a deeper, quieter and more powerful voice, a voice that is not attached to material possessions, ego identifications, social affirmation, tribal inclusion, a voice that does not care about how others see us. It is through the voice of the observer self that our deepest and greatest level of awareness, connection and truth speaks to us.

Our observer self, the ego antidote

The observer self, as we have seen, belongs not to our temporary human self that is always striving to find its identity, but to our eternal self that at all times knows our true identity, our true purpose and our deepest desires. The observer self does not deal with emotions; it is not interested in sadness or joy as both of these are merely temporary. The observer self does not deal in shame or guilt, it has no emotional fear, it simply tells us the truth or it asks us the real questions we need to answer. Sometimes people tell me that I ask them hard questions about their life and whether they are actually happy in their job, their marriage, and so on, and I always reply that there are no hard questions – questions are simply questions – it's the answers that are difficult. Likewise, the observer self does not ask hard questions or emotional questions – it simply asks honest and important questions; it's our answers that can cause resistance and struggle.

Using the observer self

Very often we can be aware of the thoughts in our head, we can listen to them, at times we can even laugh at them. Have you ever wondered what part of you is listening to these thoughts in your head? What part of you is at times able to hear a thought or a command from your brain and yet not act on it? The observing self is that part of us that is able to 'watch, observe and witness' the thinking self without judgement or reaction, knowing that all our thoughts are not necessarily true or important or worth getting attached to. Our observer self allows us to examine, change and regulate our thinking and emotional response. Engaging the observer self gives us the ability to observe ourselves and ask if our emotional reaction is enabling us or disabling us, healing us or hurting us. By actively observing our reactions we can disengage from unhelpful or hurtful, self-limiting reactions more quickly and in doing so engage the greatest choice and freedom we have, which is to choose how we respond to any given situation.

Activating the observer self allows us to become the conscious response and the conscious co-creator of our life and no longer the unconscious reflex. One of the greatest and most powerful shifts we can make in our awareness and our consciousness is to move from the belief that we are victims, people *to* whom life happens, and instead see ourselves as people *for* whom life happens. So we stop asking, 'Why is this happening *to* me?' and we start to ask a far more empowered question, 'Why is this happening *for* me?' Once we bring this new level of awareness and observation to our responses, we can stop ourselves from falling back into old unhelpful or hurtful patterns.

Our observer self is not trying to support, uphold or defend any beliefs we hold. It is always open to new possibilities, new potential and new growth. It is not committed to understanding what happens in the outside world; it is committed to understanding us and why we react the way we do.

As the observer self, we would never make a statement such as 'That person is making me angry'; instead the observer self would say, 'That person has triggered the anger I am holding'. Our observer self will gradually help us separate from these automatic patterns of emotion. It can be useful to give these patterns a name. We often refer to the automatic emotional patterns as 'the lower self'. Our ability to see these automatic patterns from the observer's point of view is strengthening our connection with our higher self.

The observer self is able to hear a thought or a command from our brain yet not act on it. This concept is known as the subject/object connection. We are not victims of our thoughts or our emotions and neither

> 'We are not victims of our thoughts or our emotions and neither do we ever have to believe or act on them.'

do we ever have to believe or act on them. That is, of course, as long as we keep our awareness open and clear, and keep acting from the observer self and not the thinking/feeling self.

If the noise of the brain or the nervous system becomes too loud, we get lost in this noise and we lose our sense of greater awareness. An awakened observer self allows us always to be aware of our thoughts and emotions but it chooses whether we attach to them, act on them or give them any energy.

Overcoming our ego and waking up our observer self requires truth, and truth can be difficult

There are two main reasons why so few of us ever get to really hear this observer voice. The first is that the noise of the ego is so loud we simply can't hear anything else, and the second is that so many of us are actually afraid of hearing it as we know it will shine a light on how much striving, pretending and suppressing we are doing and how much unhealed trauma and pain we are carrying.

Because the observer self is committed to true peace, it operates only from a place of truth. It demands that we ask ourselves the deepest truths about our lives, the things we chase, the person we pretend to be. And very often people choose to sedate themselves with a lie rather than awaken themselves with the truth because staying sedated is easy, it's familiar and it requires little change, whereas waking up requires growth and growing pains and it requires letting go of everything that is familiar and safe. Listening to and acknowledging our deepest truth requires us to finally stand and face our pain in order to heal it. Numbing and suppressing pain is what the ego is best at, but numbing and suppressing pain is not healing it. The ego wants us to suppress and numb; the observer self wants us to face and feel and then release so we can be free. We need to become aware of the stories and labels our ego is feeding us, and then challenge and rise above them. We are not our past. We are not the decisions we made yesterday. We are free beings, free to make new and better decisions any time we want.

Thinking is temporary, awareness is permanent

We are not always thinking: there are moments when our mind is clear, be it for a second or a minute; there are moments that are free from conscious thoughts. But even in these moments there is an awareness. Thoughts come and go; the process of thinking starts and stops but awareness is constant. The most constant part of our being is our awareness.

Press Pause

Place your index finger on the very top of your nose, just beneath your forehead. Press the finger in gently and wait for the next thought. You might very well find that as you are waiting, and your intention is on the waiting, for that moment there is no thought, but there is an awareness. Awareness is our eternal form of existence; thoughts and emotions are the temporary sensations that arrive and go according to temporary situations.

When the observer self is activated, we can shift our awareness from our point of pain to our point of power. We now have the awareness to recognise where we are perpetuating our own suffering, to decide not to engage with it and instead to choose the emotion we want to be experiencing. We choose our place of power, not our place of pain.

Emotional freedom happens when we have the courage to switch on our observer self, become aware of the emotion rising in us and give that emotion the freedom it requires to surface. Then, as our observer self, we can observe the emotion without judgement and ask the second most important question: 'What is the root cause of this emotion?'

Identifying the emotion is the first step towards under-standing the root cause of the emotion, which, as we have seen in Secion 1, often has something to do with the past, or beliefs, or thinking, or expectations. That which has triggered the emotion is our teacher.

Awakening the observer self

Awakening the observer self involves developing self-awareness and cultivating a detached perspective towards our thoughts, emotions and behaviours. Here are some steps you can take to awaken your observer self:

1. Practise mindfulness: Mindfulness involves paying attention to the present moment without judgement. Engage in regular mindfulness meditation or daily practices like focused breathing, body scans or mindful movements to train your mind to observe thoughts and feelings without getting caught up in them.

2. Cultivate self-reflection: Set aside time for self-reflection regularly, where you can review your experiences, actions and patterns of thinking. Ask yourself questions that encourage awareness and understanding, such as 'Why did I react that way?' or 'What are my underlying motivations?'

3. Develop self-compassion: It's important to approach self-observation with kindness and understanding. Treat yourself with compassion and avoid harsh self-judgement. This allows you to observe yourself objectively without excessive self-criticism.

4. Observe without attachment: When thoughts, emotions or situations arise, consciously step back and view them

from a distance. Instead of reacting automatically, observe your internal reactions and external behaviours without getting overly involved or identifying with them.

5. Practise non-identification: Recognise that you are not defined solely by your thoughts, emotions or roles. Remind yourself that you are the sole observer of all these experiences, and that they don't define your true self. By detaching your identity from these experiences, you can foster awareness of the observer self.

6. Seek feedback from others: Get honest feedback from trustworthy friends or mentors about your behaviours, blind spots and patterns. Others often perceive aspects of us that we may miss, allowing us to gain a deeper understanding of ourselves.

7. Embrace stillness and solitude: Spend time in quiet solitude regularly to create space for self-reflection and observation. Engage in activities like journaling, taking nature walks or practising solitude and meditation to help silence the external distractions and focus inward.

Remember, awakening the observer self is an ongoing process that requires patience, consistency and self-compassion. By practising these techniques regularly, you can develop a deeper understanding of yourself, your behaviours and the patterns that influence your life.

Press Pause

Close your eyes and take a deep breath. Allow your mind to gently settle into a state of calm and presence. Now, imagine yourself stepping back from your thoughts, emotions and experiences, like a witness observing everything from a distance. This is your observer self, the part of you that remains untouched and unaffected by the outer world.

As you connect with your observer self, let go of any judgement or attachment to what you observe. Simply be aware of everything that arises within you – thoughts, feelings, bodily sensations – without getting entangled in them. Notice how your observer self remains still and serene amidst the ever-changing nature of your inner world.

With each breath, allow this observer self to awaken within you, guiding you to clarity and understanding. Through its lens, the chaotic becomes ordered, the overwhelming becomes manageable, and the unknown becomes familiar. Embrace this perspective, like a beacon of light illuminating the depths of your being.

In this state of awakened observation, you gain insight into your true nature and the infinite layers of your existence. You discover the power to detach from the dramas and distractions of daily life, and instead connect with a deeper level of peace and intuition.

As you continue to cultivate this observer self, remember to carry its wisdom into your daily life. Allow it to guide your actions, choices and interactions. By embracing your observer self, you unlock the true potential of your emotional health and embark on a journey of self-discovery and personal growth.

Take a final deep breath, gently bring your awareness back to the present moment, and open your eyes. Carry the essence of your observer self with you, welcoming the freedom and clarity it offers in every aspect of your life.

SUMMARY

- How we can begin to consciously change our emotional states
- The freedom choice: we can control our responses
- Moving from emotional reactions to emotional responses
- Awakening our higher awareness
- Examining the duality of our existence
- Moving beyond the thinking self and ego
- Feeding the ego, starving the soul
- Dissolving the human ego
- Thinking is temporary, awareness is permanent
- Awakening our observer self

3

The Emotional Choice

In my own life, I have not yet reached a point of enlightenment whereby I don't experience all emotions. Week to week, day by day, I find myself experiencing the full spectrum of emotions from joy and happiness to fear, anger and boredom. What matters is our ability to not get consumed by them or to act on them. I have come to realise that very often when I am in a less-serving emotional state, such as fear, anger or frustration, there is a part of me that is committed to justifying the emotion and a part of me trying to come up with reasons as to why I feel like this, and in doing so I am actually perpetuating my own negativity: I am prolonging and intensifying my own suffering. The ability to self-regulate our emotions has a really powerful impact on our mental and physical wellness, not just our health but also our ability to enjoy this one, short life as it is unfolding with greater ease and joy. Changing our emotions through conscious regulation is absolutely possible, and the ability to regulate our inner emotional state gives us an amazing opportunity to live a healthy, happy and content life where we experience far greater inner ease, peace and joy while allowing the external world to be what it needs to be and allowing other people to be who they need to be. Inner emotional regulation is one of the greatest skills and one of the greatest gifts I have given myself. In the section that follows, we will see how we can practically and powerfully begin to take control of our emotions and regulate and dissolve them in order to live a more peaceful, balanced life.

In 'The Truth About Emotions' we looked at what emotions are, why we have them, how every emotion creates chemical and physical changes in our body, and the impact emotions have on our nervous system. We also learned that our emotions can be conscious or unconscious, and we saw the danger of chronic emotional unease if we don't learn to regulate and dissolve emotions.

In 'The Awareness Shift', we explored the observer self and how the first step to emotional health and emotional freedom is the ability to observe our emotions from a higher level of awareness, without judgement or attachment. We also explored the ego and how the ego can become so loud that we lose the ability to hear our higher observer self and as a result become lost in the power of our emotions.

Now we need to learn how to become more aware of our emotions, and how we can work to dissolve and regulate them.

But in order to begin our journey, you might be surprised to hear that the first step can be letting go.

Letting go of harmful beliefs

In the first section we touched upon the beliefs we hold and the impact these have on our emotional health – our beliefs about the world and the beliefs we hold about ourselves. One of the most important steps we can take on the path to emotional freedom is letting go of these harmful beliefs and replacing them with a belief system that allows us more freedom and that is more in line with our deepest values.

Don't be afraid to be your true self

One of the most common questions I am asked in my work is how we can become less concerned about what other people think. We all live with the need to be recognised, the need to be accepted. It's normal for people to want to fit in; it's normalto want to be part of a community. However, we must remember it can become an unhealthy addiction or obsession to be overly concerned about what other people think.

'One of the most important steps we can take on the path to good emotional health and emotional freedom is letting go of these harmful beliefs and replacing them with a belief system that allows us more freedom and that is more in line with our deepest values.'

Sometimes we delay our dreams, we manipulate our actions, we limit what we say and we suppress our inner truths for fear of rejection. Very often in life we value social acceptance more than self-expression.

The more we control what we say and hide our inner beliefs, the more unhappy we will be because we are suppressing our true self, masking our true beauty,

'A suppressed soul leads to a suppressed life.'

limiting our infinite potential, and by suppressing these we are amputating our soul, which is the very essence of who we are and the very thing that makes us come alive. A suppressed soul leads to a suppressed life. We need to move beyond this idea of conditional love and fear.

The most important thing is that we are truly and uniquely ourselves, and that we give ourselves permission to express ourselves and our truths in an open and honest way. The more we allow people to be who they need to be, the more we gain the courage, the strength, the wisdom and the permission to be who we need to be. Self-expression, expression of our deepest, truest self, is the deepest, truest gift.

Press Pause

The questions are: Who am I today? What is it my soul is asking me to leave behind? What is it that I dream of now? What dreams and ambitions have I outgrown? What no longer motivates me? What no longer nourishes my soul? There comes a time when we realise we outgrow our tribe, we outgrow certain dreams and ambitions, and that the path to emotional health and emotional freedom is allowing ourselves to redefine ourselves and to challenge harmful beliefs.

Take some time to journal and use the above questions as a catalyst to help you ignite, restart and realign you on your life path.

Observe your reaction to and interpretation of other people's actions and words

Another important way to challenge and change our unconscious beliefs is to become aware of how we interpret other people's reactions towards us. If we have a deep belief that we're not good enough, or not funny, or that people don't like us, then no matter how people react on the outside, we will interpret their reactions in a way that suits our deepest beliefs. It is amazing how we can manipulate other people's actions and words to match our inner beliefs.

In the section on unconscious emotions, we looked at how external stimuli can set off emotional reactions. In the same way, an external event such as a simple comment can have a trigger effect on our deepest-held beliefs and values, causing us to react in a certain way. Earlier, we used the example of the work colleague asking for a report that was due. If a key value of ours is professionalism and our ability to do our job, this question will have a deep impact on us as it calls into question a belief we hold about ourselves.

In order to begin living with more freedom, we need to fact-check our interpretations in different situations:

- Am I interpreting a person's actions, words and behaviours in a way that simply suits my unconscious programs?

- Do I tend to end up at a point where the things other people say and do are always bringing me back to a similar theme, such as I am not good enough, I am not clever enough, I am not worthy enough?

When we ask ourselves these questions we may realise that so many different situations, actions and comments by so many people have been manipulated by us in order to reinforce an inner belief. When we check our stories and fact-check our interpretations to really test their truth we can begin to believe in new things and new ways.

Establishing new beliefs about the people in our lives: the freedom contract

We all, at times, lose so much time and happiness because other people don't act the way we want them to act or respond in the way we want them to respond, especially if they are family. But the truth is we can often hold these high expectations of other people without any agreement ever being made.

We don't have contracts with family – we don't have an agreed contract with siblings as to how they should react when we need them, or how Mum or Dad should behave simply because they have a label of Mum or Dad. We superimpose labels and expectations onto other people, and the moment we do, we are setting ourselves up for suffering. Of course, that is not to say that it is wrong to expect love and respect from people you hold dear and from people you see as primary caregivers – this optimism is what drives us to pursue deep and meaningful relationships. The point I am making here is not about what we expect from relationships: it's about what we expect from the people we are in relationships with, especially when these are people that we don't necessarily choose to form a relationship with. Once we become aware that someone doesn't or can't meet our emotional needs and expectations, we can do the following. (1) Have an open and honest conversation, without blame or judgement, with them, where the focus is not on their behaviour but on the impact their behaviour is having on us and how it makes us feel; explain and name both our emotional needs and our disappointments and hope this new awareness will either allow us to see their behaviour in a new way or allow them to change their behaviour. (2) If we have done this and they simply can't or don't want to engage, then this is when we release our expectations from them. We can't expect something from someone that they are not capable of giving or committed to giving and, if we do, we are setting ourselves up for constant disappointment.

Expanding, evolving and changing our deepest beliefs

There are many ways we can begin to change our beliefs. Our subconscious beliefs are the stories that are constantly running through our minds even though we are not consciously aware of them. Every experience we have has to be passed through and interpreted by our subconscious beliefs and that is why we say that we don't experience the world

'That is why we say that we don't experience the world as it is: we experience the world as we are.'

as it is: we experience the world as we are; we experience the world through the quality and lens of our subconscious beliefs. As mentioned earlier, if our emotional and attachment needs were met as a child, we will likely experience the presence of a more positive belief system about ourselves and the world but very often the beliefs that speak the loudest are the ones that are fear based.

Negative subconscious beliefs can create self-sabotage, a loud inner critic, anger, jealousy and procrastination. To get to know our subconscious beliefs, we begin by looking at our predominant patterns and habits and see, at the moments that these habits happen, what was the emotion we were experiencing, what was the inner story we were telling and what was the belief these were linked to. For many of us this can be:

- What if this doesn't work out?
- I will never be able for that.
- What if I make a fool of myself?
- What if I get hurt?
- What if this person abandons me?

The emotions most associated with these beliefs are shame, guilt, fear and anxiety.

The good news is we can change them and we can create a mindset where our natural tendency is to look to opportunity not threat and to abundance not scarcity. One method to do this is very easy but powerful: it is simply changing our stories. The words we use and the stories we tell ourselves play a vital role in forming our subconscious beliefs. The more often we tell ourselves the same (or a similar) story, regardless of whether the story is true or has any evidence in reality, the more it is believed by the subconscious programs and submitted to our subconscious beliefs.

Develop the habit of challenging doubt

Another easy way to change our subconscious beliefs is to learn how to challenge self-doubt. To do this, we must become aware of how many times we doubt ourselves, and as soon as we begin to doubt we must stop, take a deep breath and challenge that doubt:

- Is it true?
- Have I any evidence of this?
- Is this just me limiting myself?
- Is anyone else actually saying this about me?
- Has this ever been done by somebody else?

Sometimes to challenge self-doubt we simply need to ask ourselves a more challenging question. Instead of asking, *Will this work out?* we should ask something like:

- If I really didn't care about other people's opinions, what decision would I make?
- If I absolutely had to make this work out, what would I do?
- If I had to be a success, what would that look like?
- If I could be brave for 20 seconds, what would that look like?

For anybody who may not know my full story, or has not read my first book, *Awaken Your Power Within*, I think it is important here to talk about a really crucial time in my life, a time that would go on to inform every big decision. When I was 24 years old I found myself suddenly rushed to hospital with suspected pericarditis. I was struggling to breathe, struggling to walk, and for a number of days I really thought I was going to die.

For anybody who has ever faced that situation, where we come face to face with our own mortality and the shortness of life, we realise at that moment what's important. For me, I realised that much of what I had spent my time chasing, the things I thought were important, were actually not important at all. It's not until we get to the end of our life, or a point where we think our life is ending, that we come to understand that the tragedy of life is not death: the tragedy of life is arriving at the end and realising we have never lived. At 24, when I thought my life was ending, I looked back and reflected on it, and I was deeply saddened by the things I had put my time and energy into, and the things I had let go of and never pursued. The deepest regret I had at that time was the amount of love and joy that I never got to experience.

When we are faced with a situation like this, it really challenges us to ask ourselves:

- What is really important to me?
- Who is important to me?
- What are my values?
- What do I stand for?
- Why am I pursuing the things I do?

- Why are they important?
- What is the legacy I will leave behind?
- Is there enough happiness in my life?
- Is there enough love in my life?

Thankfully, I recovered, and I have always maintained that sense of perspective. I have always remembered what it is like to face mortality, and the questions and the self-reflection that brings. It is my absolute belief that when we approach the end of our lives, the only thing that really matters is the amount of love and joy we have experienced and the service we have been to others. At 24 years old I made myself a promise: regardless of what I would do, or the things I would achieve, the failures I would encounter, the people I would meet, I would pursue love and peace. I would follow my heart so that at the end of my life I would have no regrets. I would live a life of love and passion and purpose, where I had the courage to pursue my dreams, to speak my truth, to stand on my own two feet and to discover who I am.

We are now beginning to see the link between our emotions and our beliefs and how by changing our beliefs about ourselves from *I am not good enough, I am not loved, I am not worthy*, to I am enough, I am loved, I am worthy, we can begin to change our emotions. We begin to replace fear with love and we can begin to change our emotional responses.

> 'When we begin to truly understand what our deepest values and beliefs are, we can then move on to the next step of living with true emotional freedom and good emotional health.'

When we train our mind to challenge our inner doubts, to look for evidence, we realise that most of the doubts we hold are simply self-created and have no basis in reality. When we begin to truly understand what our deepest values and beliefs are, we can then move on to the next step of living with true emotional freedom and good emotional health.

Re-priming our reticular activating system

The words we use and the stories we tell ourselves also play a very important role in a special part of the brain called the reticular activating system. The role of the reticular activating system is to make sure that we are at all times consciously aware of the things that are of importance to us – to the detriment of the things it thinks are not important to us. If something is defined by the reticular activating system as not important, we actually become consciously blind to it, and although it might be right in front of us, we are unable to see it. The only way that the reticular activating system can identify what is important to us is by listening to the things we give our energy and attention to.

We know from social media that the more interest we have in something, the more we click on or like that particular topic. That expression of interest forms an algorithm that tells the social media platform what we are interested in, and so more of that topic and others like it, more information, images and videos, begin to appear in our feed. While this type of content becomes more prominent in our feed, the things we don't express an interest in are gradually taken off our feed, until eventually they disappear completely. We are literally creating an echo chamber.

The reticular activating system of the brain is something similar. It is constantly listening to what we talk about, what we think about and what we listen to. Because we are investing so much of our time and attention into these things, the reticular activating system begins to believe that these are what are most important to us and so it allows the conscious mind only to become aware of the cues in the external world that match this inner interest. Consequently, we become hyper-focused on certain cues in our external world and we become consciously blind to many other things. This means that our subconscious beliefs are constantly being affirmed and never challenged.

We all know that the more we think about something, the more it seems to appear in our outside world. The more we think about red cars, the more we begin to see red cars. But the truth is, of course, that those red cars haven't just appeared in our outside world; they were always there. We were consciously unaware of them until we started to think about them and speak about them and the moment we did that, the moment we invested our mental energy in them, the more we became consciously aware of their existence. In order to change our unconscious programs, we must begin to change our inner stories. We must begin to prime our reticular activating system with new images, new visions and new stories.

We must begin to prime our conscious mind with new cues. The more we change our stories, the more we realign and refocus our reticular activating system, the more we begin to see new evidence of great opportunities that maybe we didn't believe in in the past. The more we begin to search for evidence of our own genius, our own ability and our own potential, the more we begin to witness it. Changing the direction and the priming of our reticular activating system plays a massive role in changing our deepest beliefs.

The various ways we can prime our reticular activating system are:

1. Vision board: A physical board that contains powerful images and words that are directly connected to the opportunities we want more of. Visualisation, where we bring to life the clear details of the things we want, is a really powerful tool we can use.

2. Powerful affirmations: Our reticular activating system is listening to everything we say out loud or in our mind so repeating powerful words and directing our communication towards the things we want more of is a powerful way of priming it.

3. Loading everyday habits: When we are doing everyday activities like brushing our teeth we can place cards with positive suggestions on the mirror and repeat the statements while we are brushing our teeth. We spend so much time on everyday tasks that when we begin to use them as positive priming moments we greatly speed up the process.

**AFFIRMATIONS TO HELP ESTABLISH
NEW BELIEFS ABOUT YOURSELF**

1. I am enough.
2. I am loved.
3. I deserve abundance and it will find me easily.
4. I adapt easily to life's changes.
5. I trust that everything will make sense in the end.
6. I can let go of the past that no longer serves me.
7. I welcome uncertainty and the unknown as a beautiful opportunity.

Press Pause

Changing deep-rooted beliefs and thought patterns can be hard. It takes presence, consciousness and practice to catch yourself when you are falling back into subconscious beliefs about yourself. Here are a couple of examples of negative thought patterns and stories we might tell ourselves and how we can switch them up:

Inner script: I failed that test/exam/job interview. I really am not good enough at anything.

Replace with: I'm proud of myself for trying. Not everyone can do that. I am proud of myself for showing up and doing my best.

Inner script: I let that person down. I wasn't there for them when they needed me. I am a terrible, selfish person.

Replace with: What were the reasons I couldn't be there for that person? I know I am not a terrible person because I feel bad that I wasn't there. There must be something going on with me that prevented me from being there for that person. I owe it to myself to figure out what this is and to help myself.

Slowing down to meet your emotional edge

I believe we now live in a world where we suffer from the disease of fast. We have ample amounts of 15 minute workouts, 8 minute workouts and 5 minute workouts. We have 5 minute meals, 2 minute meals and everything is telling us to do things quicker and quicker. At times this is perfectly fine. At times we only have that 10 or 15 minutes. However, very often when we're doing things fast we mask or we miss the things that are really important, things like the deep emotions that we're holding, the pain that the body is trying to express, the message that the body is trying to communicate. This vital information gets lost because of the speed at which we're living; the speed hides our emotional needs. This happens to us all at times and although I was unaware it had happened to me I was about to find out. I was about to discover yin yoga and through slowing down I would meet my emotional edge. The ability to bring ourselves to this emotional edge, where our deepest emotions and emotional wounds exist, and not to run away is an essential part of gaining emotional freedom.

'Speed hides our emotional needs.'

As part of rediscovering my emotional health and reigniting my inner passion and joy, I knew I had to try something new. In order to have what we have never had and in order to feel how we have never felt, we have to be willing to do something we have never done. I looked at all my own practices – exercise, cold-water immersion, meditation, diet – and while all these have been extremely powerful in my life and have brought me incredible clarity, calmness and joy, it was as though I had reached a new level of awareness and to move beyond that I needed to introduce something new.

It is important for all of us to regularly look at our practices and remember that because we are continuously changing, our practices need to adapt to our current state of thinking, feeling and being, and they need to be in line with our current desires. The more we do things, the more they become unconscious, the less likely we are to have a conscious breakthrough while doing them. If we are regularly changing our thinking we must regularly upgrade our actions and practices. It doesn't mean that we have to let go of all the old practices. I knew that my practices were fundamental to my emotional health and so I knew they had to remain as my anchor practices, but as I moved through my emotional healing, deep down I felt it was time to add a new practice that could potentially take me to a new level of feeling and awareness. As it turned out, that practice was yin yoga.

I have been doing yoga for many years now. For me, it's an amazing time to clear my mind, a moving meditation, but I also love the physical challenge. Exercise for me is a way to focus my mind and it's vital for my mental health, but the competitive side of me also wants to get the most physically out of my training sessions and yoga practice. Many of us are the same: we will look at how long the class is and ask things like *Will I get a good workout? Will I get my heart rate up? How many calories will I burn?* If there is a 15 minute class that ticks these boxes then that's the one; if there is a 5 minute one then that's even better: get the hit, get it done, get out.

I learned that this attitude is often the opposite of what real health and balance is about.

I had been to numerous types of yoga classes and as I headed to my first yin yoga class I was expecting 60 minutes of challenging poses to give my mind and body a good stretch and some meditation at the end to help me centre and align mind, body and spirit. On the way to the class my subconscious mind wanted to double check that I was going into the familiar, because our ego loves familiarity.

So I asked my wife, 'Is this like regular yoga?'

'Yes and no,' she replied, smiling. 'It's 90 minutes and in that 90 minutes you will do four or five poses max.'

'How is it so slow?' I asked.

'That's the purpose of it,' she said, 'it's slow for a reason.'

I have to admit my first reaction was *Do I have time for 90 minutes? Would I be better off jumping on the treadmill and getting a 'good' workout?*

But I was committed, so I decided I would give it a shot. But already somewhere in my mind I had concluded that it wasn't for me. I needed something faster. Speed, powering through and getting things done had been my way of operating for the previous few months. We had just had our second baby, our business was expanding, we had moved to a different country. There was much change and uncertainty. I felt a lot of responsibility on my shoulders to make the best decisions for my family and our future. I didn't want any self-doubt creeping in. I buried all my doubt and uncertainty by keeping busy, keeping going – never allowing myself to show the vulnerability that comes with any change: man up, toughen up, be strong.

I was experiencing a lot of frustration at the time – things not working out as I had wanted them to during our move. Looking back, I was stressed and operating from my sympathetic nervous system. But what I know now is that the speed hides the need, and the more my emotional needs and suppressed emotions bubbled up, the more I ran from them. The more I speeded up and the busier I became and the more I did, the more my nervous system released cortisol and adrenaline and this was now keeping me in a state of fight-or-flight where the easiest thing to do was just to keep going. But as we now know, that only leads to emotional and physical destruction. When we are in this state of speed with this addiction to adrenaline we are like anyone with a craving: they know it's bad for them, they can feel its damage at every level of their being but they don't know how to stop it. We can become addicted to speed and to fast, fast, fast.

Yin yoga is about slowing down so that we can truly feel and listen to our own inner needs. It's about connecting to our deepest self, to our deepest body, and becoming aware of what's actually happening in our body and mind. By doing this, by slowing down, we are able to hear the key messages that our body, our organs and our mind are trying to tell us. When we slow down, we activate the parasympathetic nervous system, and when we do, we switch on our healing. We cannot switch on our parasympathetic nervous system if we're doing things fast, fast, fast.

Thankfully I was about to meet the person who would put my brakes on. The class started and the teacher let us know that we would be moving through 5 poses and holding each pose for 5 or 10 minutes. There was something inside me that was still saying, 'This is too slow for me, I will be bored.' But I was there, so I decided to immerse myself in the class. Tomorrow, I vowed, I would go to the gym and get back on the treadmill for a 'good' workout.

The teacher began to guide us into our first pose. Slowly we held and stabilised the pose, then slowly … deepen and hold … then deepen … And suddenly any expectation I had of being bored was gone. From somewhere there ignited a deeper level of focus. I became very awake and as I felt the physical discomfort of the deep pose my initial reaction was to pull out of it, to pull away from the discomfort. But just before I did the teacher began to speak. It was like she was listening to my thoughts. She encouraged us to acknowledge whatever discomfort we may be experiencing and try not to run away from it but to accept it, not judge it or label it as right or wrong but instead just use it as information from the body and listen to what the body was saying.

For too long I had forgotten the importance of listening to my body. Every day our body sends us signs and critical information and feedback and all too often we are just not listening. Too many times our body sends us information about the food we are eating but we ignore it or switch it off by taking medication. Heartburn is the body's way of sending us crucial information that we need to change our food or our lifestyle but we take a heartburn tablet and carry on as we have been doing. We get a headache and without asking anything about the headache or the important signal our body is sending us we take the headache tablet and again we are saying to the body, *Shut up.*

In this instance, my yin practice was forcing me to slow down, to reconnect to my body. My body was crying out for rest. My nervous system was trying to rebalance. During our move, when things didn't work out as I wanted them to, I felt impatience and frustration. Of course, it's simply impossible to control everything, but the more out of control things were, the more I perceived this as failing and this manifested itself in high levels of stress. It is important to note that we can express emotions in different ways and we can disguise them to ourselves but when we really listen and feel them the truth will appear.

In the yin class, the teacher instructed us to continue to listen, to use our breath to soften both our mind and our body, and as soon as I focused on my breath, as soon as I stopped resisting the pose and the discomfort and started to meet it with curiosity, something else began to appear, something remarkable. I began to realise that as I moved beyond my physical resistance to the poses, behind this physical resistance was a powerful emotion. Anger. I couldn't believe the amount of anger that was bubbling up. *Where is this coming from?* I asked myself. My initial reaction was to try and stop it, change it, deny it. But once again, as if the teacher was listening to my thoughts, she gently asked us to become aware of the emotion we were beginning to experience and to not run from it or label it or judge it, to simply allow it to surface and allow it to dissolve.

As I held that pose over the next few minutes, the anger I didn't even know I was carrying came to the surface. It became clear that for the last few months I'd been simply distracting and suppressing my emotions. I had been directing all of my frustration and anger towards the things that went wrong with our move. When I really drilled down and faced my emotions, it became obvious to me that this anger had been building in me because of the challenges I was facing as a dad. The life readjustment since we'd had our two children had been immense. Everyone spoke about how wonderful fatherhood was, full of heart-blowing love, but I felt like I was failing my wife and I was failing my children. This reignited my inner critic. For a while, I felt frustrated, impatient towards the huge changes my life had undergone – changes that meant I could no longer live the life I used to live.

But deep down, the real issue was that becoming a dad meant that I was no longer in control, and this had made me feel like a failure. Becoming a dad also made me revisit my old demons and deepest beliefs and how I felt as a child. What we now know from trauma is that old hurts can reappear when we encounter situations that trigger us back to past wounds. The anger I was feeling about all the change that was happening in my life was not about the hiccups we experienced during our move, it was about my feelings as a dad and my anger at myself that I was letting my family down.

Becoming a dad in many ways was an experience that made me examine my deepest wounds and also made me very aware that I did not want to pass these wounds on to my children. Intergenerational trauma is a fascinating study and a fascinating way of exploring the unconscious hurts and wounds that are handed down to us by our parents and that can resurface again when we become parents ourselves. As my eldest son got a little older, I found that I was responding to his emotional needs from my own emotional wounds. As a child I was quiet, sensitive, an overthinker and a worrier. When I got upset as a child I felt overwhelmed and often frightened. Now I found myself reacting to my son's upset as though he was me – a sensitive, emotional overthinker and worrier. I caught myself overcompensating when he became upset – doing whatever I could to protect him from the hurt he was feeling. I tried to chase his emotions away. But of course,

'Old hurts can reappear when we encounter situations that trigger us back to past wounds.'

he's not me, he's not the same little boy, and I needed to learn to acknowledge his emotions and to allow him that space – but I found myself projecting my emotional wounds on to him.

After that yin yoga class, I vowed that I would no longer run from my emotional wounds and unconscious emotional states. And that whatever it took for me to understand and heal these would be the greatest gift I could give my children. I would be the one to break the cycle. It was time to overcome the disease and disregulation of fast.

WHAT IS EMOTIONAL DISSOCIATION?

Emotional disassociation is where the body tries to protect itself against emotions it can't handle. It creates an emotional barrier between the pain and itself. It can separate us physically and chemically from those emotions by constructing a wall, a screen, a mask behind which it can hide those emotions. In the short term of course this can be positive; there certainly are times in which we need time and space to try to get through the immediate aftermath and the immediate pain before we can begin to deal with the deeper, bigger emotions.

But in the long term all these emotions have to be dealt with. If we don't face them, not only do we suppress and numb the painful emotions and memories, we also suppress and deny all of the memories that we might associate with them, even if they are positive. Sometimes to numb the pain we must also numb the joy. Understanding, resolving and creating new emotional triggers allows us to dissolve the pain and experience the joy. Far too many times in my life when I was at my lowest I told myself to toughen up, to man up. From all my years of discovery and gaining incredible freedom from trauma, I am more certain than ever that being strong is absolutely not about being tough or toughening up. In fact it is the total opposite. In the softening of my emotions I had the incredible ability to meet my pain with gentleness and non-resistance, and in doing so I learned how to see them as signposts to my greatest healing.

All through the class, in every pose, the teacher encouraged us to meet our discomfort without judgement or labels and to meet every emotion with kindness because we were meeting our deepest self. She encouraged us to become comfortable in the discomfort because life will not always be comfortable, it will not always be easy, and if we run from, suppress or deny the discomfort we will either live a life of always being in our comfort zone, our familiar, our known and our past, and never really be able to move beyond it, or we will spend our life running away from everything that challenges us. Becoming comfortable in the discomfort was my new mantra and to meet every emotion without judgement or label became the task. And to understand that in meeting our deepest emotions we are meeting our real state of self was an awakening that could have taken me years of reading and a lifetime of thinking about, yet here in the 90 minute class I was shown the gateway that would lead to my next level of emotional freedom.

In this yoga class, the teacher brought us to our emotional edge, and instead of recoiling and running away from the discomfort she allowed us to breathe into it, to soften into it, to listen to it and to move through it. We often think that breakthrough is about force, but here in yin yoga I was beginning to realise that the biggest breakthroughs have actually little to do with force. It's the opposite. In order to break through, sometimes we need to soften into, to feel, to dissolve and to move through with ease, and when we do we don't just move an emotion, we actually dissolve it.

When we get into a new pose, or a pose that we find a little difficult, there is a point at which the stretch moves from easy to discomfort and the discomfort is just before the point of pain. In that scenario – just as we feel the discomfort, just before the point of pain – most of us would begin to breathe quicker, clench our jaw, tighten our face, tense up. This is sending an important message to the body that I don't like this. This is a threat, and I need to get out of here. Very quickly, as with everything in life, our body will follow our mind's command and we will pull ourselves out of that position and tell ourselves it was too deep, that it wasn't for me, I don't have that flexibility, I don't like that stretch, I'm not good at that – and by listening to those stories we are only learning how to stay in our place of comfort.

One of the biggest lessons I have learned from my practice

of yin yoga is the ability to put myself into a place of discomfort and to become comfortable in the discomfort. Yin yoga has granted me a gift where I can ease into my emotional edge and instead of retreating from it, instead of recoiling from it, instead of putting myself into a defensive mode, I have the ability to sit and breathe in that place of discomfort and listen to both the critical information my body is giving me and, more importantly, the important message about the deepest emotions I am holding.

Only when we give ourselves the opportunity to sit and be in that place of discomfort and to go beyond fear can we allow ourselves to meet our own pain and in meeting it we can now begin to hear it, understand it and dissolve it.

To become the observer of our inner emotional discomfort, we must be able to meet and feel all our emotions without judgement or criticism, or without the need to run away from this discomfort. When we no longer see these emotions and memories as a threat but instead see them as vital information, we can begin to recognise them as something to be listened to, to be learned from, things we need to resolve and dissolve, not things we need to act on or live in. Now we see them an opportunity, an invitation to ease into our emotional edge and then dissolve beyond it.

We begin to feel something at a deeper level. We realise that behind and underpinning the physical discomfort is an emotion. Yin yoga taught me that because so many of the emotions we carry are impacting our physical body and movement, if we are tight in the mind we will be tight in the body. The practice has shown me that in my own life at times when I was coming to the place of my greatest opportunity to learn and grow, just at that place of emotional discomfort I would run away.

Let's use the example of bereavement. Many people who've experienced bereavement will use lots of coping and defence mechanisms such as distraction, keeping busy – anything to stop them from sitting in that ultimate place of pain. Often they are simply too scared to allow themselves to feel their emotional pain for fear of what it will bring up or for the loss of emotional control they may experience. And while at first this is totally acceptable, eventually there comes a time when even the emotions of the greatest loss have to be acknowledged and treated with kindness and love.

Most of my biggest breakthroughs in life, from a psychological or emotional point of view, came about when I eased myself into my emotional edge, simply sitting with it, instead of running or recoiling from it. I have allowed myself to experience the discomfort through the power of the breath, the power of forgiveness, the power of non-attachment, non-resistance and non-judgement. And by becoming at ease in the discomfort, the discomfort was no longer a threat, no longer my enemy; it became my greatest learning, my greatest opportunity, my greatest friend. It became an opportunity to grow.

Press Pause

Can you think of something in your life that you are resisting? Something that is causing you discomfort? It could be a new challenge, such as a new job. It could be the risk and vulnerability of opening yourself up to love. It could be the idea of taking up a new hobby or sport that you've never tried before and you don't know if you'll be any good at. What is preventing you from moving through the discomfort of that new experience? What is preventing you from sitting with it and within it? Fear? Shame? A feeling of not being enough? Can you begin to examine what lies behind this discomfort? What emotions need to be dissolved so that you can move through discomfort to open yourself to new experiences and to live with more of a sense of ease in who you are? What would happen if you allowed yourself to open up to the discomfort, to the embarrassment of trying something new, to the risk of failing?

Breakthroughs don't have to be massive life-changing moments; they are not about physical push or force. My experience is that my greatest breakthroughs, my greatest moments, have been where I've sat without judgement or attachment and allowed myself to dissolve into and through my unconscious emotional states. When we move beyond that unconscious emotion we begin to learn who we truly are.

Dissolving our deepest-held emotional default mode or unconscious emotions takes time, practice and patience. It takes forgiveness and it takes love. But doing so is one of the most important parts of the journey to emotional health.

Giving ourselves time and space to ease into and dissolve through our emotional edge is one of the biggest gifts we can give ourselves, our health and our happiness. If we meet our emotional edge with force it becomes solid and repels us. Think of someone falling into water: even though water is soft, if someone hits it at speed and at the wrong angle the water becomes solid and it can shatter and disintegrate anything that hits it. But if we enter the water with gentleness the water meets us with gentleness, and there is no hurt and no destruction. The same applies when we meet our inner reservoir of suppressed emotions.

For so many of us the moment we start to get close, the moment we sit into that place of discomfort, we quickly recoil and our coping mechanisms kick in, which might be to distract ourselves or to use social media or alcohol or to make light of the situation. These coping mechanisms are what I call our emotional stabilisers.

Taking off our emotional stabilisers

In order to harness this power of true emotional health, we must be willing to leave the harbours of the old, the safe and the familiar and to step with awareness into our emotional freedom. There is a beautiful expression that says ships are safe in the harbour, but that is not what ships are built for. The ship has a harbour and we as human beings have emotional safe zones or what I like to call emotional stabilisers. When a child cycles a bike with stabilisers the child may think they've learned how to cycle but the truth is they have only learned how to cycle with stabilisers. When they begin to gather speed and take off, they might experience a wobble, and they lean on the stabilisers for support. But with stabilisers on, they will never learn how to balance or cycle properly.

Similarly, in life, we can rely on our emotional stabilisers. Remember, the ego wants to keep us locked in the familiar. The thinking brain finds safety in fear, doubt, uncertainty and anger as these are the states that protect us from the world. If we don't show weakness, if we're not vulnerable and if we don't open ourselves to other people, we will keep ourselves safe but opening ourselves up completely to life is where we will find our deepest joy. Take for example somebody who dreams of starting their own business. They have an intention, an image, a vision that says I would like to start my own business, but that dream is too big and it frightens them. Instead of leaning into the uncertainty, fear overtakes ambition, doubt overcomes passion: they have leaned back onto their emotional stabilisers. We all develop circular inner thought patterns such as: *It's too hard. I would like to have weekends off. I would like to have a dependable, reliable salary. I would like to have a safe pension. I don't want to manage other people. I don't want to deal with failure if it doesn't work out.* These are all valid concerns, and some people's values lie in

'Where our attention and energy flows, our life goes.'

stability and predictability. But if we are unhappy in our life, if we feel restless and that there's something more 'out there' and we find that we are falling back on harmful emotional stabilisers, maybe

> **'We never know how strong we are until strong is the only option.'**

now is the time to really look at the unconscious emotions, the emotional stabilisers that are holding us back. Where our attention and energy flows, our life goes.

Are we truly willing to dare? Are we truly willing to believe and are we truly willing to commit? There is a wonderful expression that says the main reason why plan A doesn't work is because of the existence of plan B. Before we set off on the bicycle of life, we make sure the stabilisers are there, and when the stabilisers are there and we know they're there, we're focused on them. The first moment the bike wobbles, we lean back into safety and let the stabilisers do the work. What I've learned in my own life, a life where I've had to change my thinking, my beliefs, the nature of my business and clients, and risk it all again and again, is that unless I'm totally free and without stabilisers, I will never really find out if I can cycle or not. Unless we are truly free from emotional support, and restrictions, we may never know what is possible. They say we never know how strong we are until strong is the only option.

Modern stabilisers

Many people require external voices and external support to give them direction as to when to move, how far to move, when to sleep, how to sleep. We are constantly giving away our inner power and forget to rely on our inner instinct and wisdom. We go to the gym and allow a treadmill or a clock to decide how fast we run. But maybe we are limiting ourselves. Do we feel safer chasing a goal that we know is possible to achieve, something that everybody else is achieving? Do we need an external voice or an external tool to assure us, to motivate us? What are we really pacing ourselves for? Who are we pacing ourselves against? And in this one short, beautiful, incredible life where we are more powerful than we possibly can imagine, are we willing to take off the stabilisers, take away supports and networks that keep us linked to the past – to the thinking brain that is focused on fear, doubt, uncertainty, our unmet emotional needs – and keep us restricted by our environment? If our emotional connection is to our emotional stabilisers, then nothing will change in our life. But if we are willing to take the risk, to open ourselves to everything life has to offer, the only way we can be free from our emotional stabilisers is to meet and dissolve our emotions and therefore be able to move past our emotional edge.

Emotional triggers: how they work and how we can use them for our benefit

A short while ago I was in a European city to speak at a conference, and I met up with an ex-client of mine, a world champion in their sport, who also happened to be there at the same time. I had worked with this athlete for several years as they prepared for the world championships. As you can imagine, becoming a world champion is an extraordinary moment for any athlete, the culmination of years of dreaming, sacrifices, setbacks and overcoming adversity for that one very special moment. It is a moment so powerful, it can last a lifetime. It was the first time we had met in person in many years.

We had agreed to meet in a hotel and as they walked into the lobby we immediately embraced in an incredible hug that acknowledged the journey we had been on together, the moments we'd shared and the memories we'd created. It was like we were immediately back to where we'd left off all those years earlier and the ease of our relationship and our conversation just picked back up straight away.

As we spoke about our new lives and careers and our children, we realised how much had happened since we had last met.

'It seems like another lifetime ago,' the athlete said. 'Sometimes I can't really remember it.'

We all know how life can get so busy and can change, so much so that it isn't unusual that a part of our life can seem as though it was a lifetime ago.

Then they said something that intrigued me. 'Sometimes when I think of the world championships it seems like it was someone else who did it – it's like I am remembering someone else winning it. I can remember bits of it and I can remember the final but I can't always feel it: it's like it was someone else.'

This can be a very normal experience, but something in their eyes told me that this was causing them sadness, it was like they were trying to remember it but couldn't, so I decided to take a chance. I asked them if they had an hour for a bit of fun and, thankfully, they had. I knew that we were an easy taxi ride from where they had become world champion. 'Let's go back to the stadium,' I said, 'and see if it triggers any memories. We probably can't get in but maybe by standing outside we will feel something.'

So away we went. When we arrived outside the stadium the streets were busy, and the stadium seemed closed. But it was nice to see it again. All the signs and imagery were long gone. As we walked around we saw an entrance that was open and people bringing rubbish out from an event that had been held there the night before. I decided to take a chance. I told the security guard that my client had won a gold medal at the stadium and was wondering if we could go back in for a moment to see it. After a little hesitation he let us in, and as he did so, he remarked, 'Don't be too disappointed, it's gone downhill a little and not the shiny new place you might remember.' We went in and walked out at the top of the seating area, and from that height we had a great view of the arena. It was cold, dark and clearly in need of some cleaning after the event the night before.

As we stood there in silence, the memories started to come back, and as they did, the cold, empty arena in front of us was transforming. I could hear the packed crowd, and TV cameras and the media started to reappear, slowly, piece by piece. In my mind the arena was transforming back to the morning of the race, and as it did, little things that I thought I had forgotten came back as clear as day. I remembered arriving at the venue on the bus, the conversation we were having, coming through the security area. And then I remembered the joke the security staff member made as we were coming through. It was as though a million-piece jigsaw had been reassembled and some of the pieces that were falling into place were ones that I thought I had forgotten about – or at least consciously forgotten about, because of course we never forget anything unconsciously. It was like each big piece gave way to a smaller piece, and once I started to remember the bigger moments, such as the security area, I could then remember the face of the security guard, and once I remembered that I could remember the joke he told us. It was like a cascade of memories all being released after the floodgates were opened, and of course that is exactly how memory works.

I then turned to the athlete to see if they were having a similar experience, and as soon as I did, I realised that they were, perhaps an even deeper one. They were standing motionless, with an expression on their face that told me they were looking into a different dimension. I could see the goosebumps on their arms, so I remained silent and just let them remember. After a few minutes without shifting their gaze they said, 'It's like I'm back. It's like it's all happening again.'

'Tell me what you feel,' I said. I deliberately didn't ask what they remembered.

'I feel goosebumps,' they replied. 'I feel the same butterflies in my stomach as I did that morning as we walked into this arena. I feel exactly like I did that morning.'

'And what do you hear?'

'I hear the crowd. I hear the chanting as we arrived because an event had just finished and people were on their feet, screaming. I can hear the voice of the announcer, I can hear the music in my headphones when I put them on, it's as if it is playing now.'

Going back into the venue that day was like arriving for the very first time – the same emotions, the same feeling. It was like the body and brain had no concept of time or space, as though they were transported back in time. And of course we know they can be.

Emotions and memories are closely connected: we tend to remember the moments to which high or important emotions are attached. As we stood there with all those memories and emotions flooding back, the entire day was playing out not just in our minds but also in our bodies, in our chemistry, because as we now know, emotions are chemical and electrical messages that stimulate physical changes and feelings in our bodies.

I asked them if they remembered the moment of their win, the moment they realised they were champion. Did they remember standing on the podium? And of course instantly the memories started to flood back. I could tell simply by looking at their body position and their facial expressions.

To remember is to make present again, to make that memory part of us again. A member is part of a group, a member is part of our body, so to re-member is to make that part of us again. Our emotions and our memories show up in our bodies and our energy fields all the time whether we are aware of it or not.

As they stood there I noticed from their body language, their facial expression, that something was changing. The memory was changing; their emotions were changing. I remained silent and simply observed this happen. Soon after I noticed tears begin to fall and it was clear that deep sadness was now taking over from deep happiness. The excitement and adrenaline and joy they were clearly remembering was now giving way to something new. The memory of their final had triggered something else.

I waited a while to allow this new emotion to appear fully, before asking, 'What are you remembering?' They remained silent for a few moments; I could see them swallowing hard, trying to speak, but there was a block, a lump in their throat.

I just waited, creating a space where this new emotion would be welcomed and not judged. Then they spoke. 'Patrick,' they said, 'I can see him, I know exactly where he was standing, I remember what he was wearing, I remember running out to him after the event, I remember the hug he gave me, I remember how he felt and how he smelt. I can smell him – it's like he is here. I remember how great a friend he was.' In almost confusion, they said, 'It's like he's standing right there.'

But of course he wasn't. Patrick was a close friend of the athlete. They were lifelong buddies, but Patrick had passed away a number of years after the championships in tragic circumstances.

It was some years since Patrick had passed away and although the athlete believed that they had processed the memory of Patrick, the loss of Patrick, although they believed that they had come to peace and come to terms with it, now that they were clearly being reminded of the emotional impact that losing their friend had on them, they began to realise the power of the emotions that were not actually processed or resolved. They thought they had dealt with the death of their friend, but they had simply suppressed or denied it or distracted themselves away from truly processing it.

Our brains and nervous systems are often simply not able to process deep emotions so they suppress them until we have the energy or the resources to deal with them. We do this because of emotion dissociation, but at some point we will have to resolve them and that requires us to unlock and meet them. But often the pain or the anticipation of the pain is so powerful that we become experts at denying and suppressing emotions to the point where we can convince ourselves that we have dealt with them.

The truth is that no matter how hard we try to suppress these emotions, no matter how hard we try to avoid triggering situations, somebody or something is going to trigger them and when they do they can create chaos and personal pain.

It was now becoming clear to me why my client was finding it so hard to remember the final, to remember the thoughts, the emotions associated with the day. It was because two events had become permanently associated with each other, where one could not be experienced without the other.

Our minds, our brains, our nervous systems learn and remember by association. If we were rejected in the past or were made to feel less than or small, then a job rejection, for example, will cause us to have more powerful feelings of shame and embarrassment. We want memories to stick so that we don't forget the lesson learned by them. If we burn our hand in a fire we will never forget that and anytime we are in front of a

'The truth is that no matter how hard we try to suppress these emotions, no matter how hard we try to avoid triggering situations, somebody or something is going to trigger them and when they do they can create chaos and personal pain.'

fire we will be triggered with fear or anxiety. This is the brain's and the body's way of making sure we don't get burned again. We are always storing information in our subconscious mind that enables us to avoid situations or people in the future that have caused us hurt in the past.

We might tell ourselves we can't remember our childhood, certain parts of our schooling or certain parts of our lives but the truth may be that we have put them in a place that is beyond our conscious recall. But this doesn't mean we are not remembering them or reliving them unconsciously; these traumas and memories can manifest themselves in how we react emotionally to different situations later in life.

To create this powerful stored memory, the brain attaches things like smells, sounds, images and emotions to memories. The more multidimensional, the more clearly and quickly we remember, and we will be instantly triggered if we encounter that smell, that sound in the future. We have all experienced hearing a song being played in a shop or restaurant and being triggered back to a time in a nightclub or to a summer of fun and adventure. Or the aroma of freshly baked bread or coffee and being brought back to, for example, our parents' house.

Memories and triggers go hand in hand. Memories are all emotionally loaded and the times, the people, the situations in our life that are most emotional are the ones we most remember.

My client was having this awakening as we stood there in the arena. I simply stepped into them and held them in a hug to let them know their emotions were welcome, valid and important and that this was an important moment. I thought we had come here to relive a great occasion but I now realised we were here to relive and to heal something completely different.

When we returned to the hotel from the stadium, we had an incredible and open conversation where they talked openly about the loss they had experienced.

My client was discovering that one of their coping mechanisms to deal with the loss of their friend was to deny the emotion, suppress the pain and the bereavement, and to do that they had to deny and suppress all other emotional and powerful moments of their past that were closely associated with the person and the event. This was to the point where they were suppressing the memory of their race. The danger was that reliving it and re-feeling meant they were likely to re-feel the pain, so both had to be emotionally shut down.

> 'Memories are all emotionally loaded and the times, the people, the situations in our life that are most emotional are the ones we most remember.'

It took the emotional trigger of the greatest day of their life to make them realise that that greatest day of their life was also deeply connected to one of the most heartbreaking experiences of their life. This explains why what should have been a moment they would remember forever, they had actually suppressed, to a point where they believed they couldn't really remember it.

Brain chunking

Our brain uses a process called chunking. Brain chunking, also known as chunking information, is a cognitive process in which information is organised and grouped into meaningful units or chunks. By chunking information, we can make it easier to remember and process complex information. The brain takes a number of pieces of information, like a sound, a smell, a voice, and it quickly links and chunks it all together. It forms a picture when the picture isn't really there; it doesn't like disorder so it will create an order and a connection whether one is there or not.

Consider trying to remember a long string of numbers: 091354782636. Instead of trying to remember each digit individually, you can chunk it into smaller groups:
- 0913
- 5478
- 2636

Now, instead of remembering 12 individual digits, you only have to remember 3 chunks. This makes it much easier to recall the information when needed.

As long as there are pieces of a picture that we have previously experienced, the brain will quickly take those individual pieces, and before we know it, we think we're looking at the picture again.

It will take a sound, a smell, an image, a situation and quickly attach them all together to relive a situation from a physical, psychological and emotional point of view. Emotional triggers are really powerful; they take us back to a previous time in our life and allow us to feel exactly how we felt then. Emotional triggers are constantly being unconsciously created, so that when we experience joy and love, we will unconsciously actively seek out more of those situations in the future, and in situations where we feel pain or hurt, we will unconsciously avoid those situations in the future. Should we encounter either of those things in the future we will feel exactly like we did when we first encountered them.

But of course we can't always avoid certain situations or people, which means we can be regularly emotionally retriggered, and when we are, the emotions reappear, not just in our mind but in our body, and we physically, physiologically and chemically are back in the same state, as though the original situation is happening over and over again. The brain has no way of processing whether it's happening in the past or in the current moment.

Consciously creating positive emotional triggers

We can create positive, powerful triggers in advance of a situation. I use this regularly with the athletes I work with; we use songs, smells and movement to trigger powerful feelings of calm and focus.

It is a simple process. At the end of a training session, when the athlete is feeling positive and powerful due to the presence of endorphins in their system, we get them to lie on the floor, slow their breathing and begin to repeat positive affirmations in their mind: *I am strong, I am powerful, I am in control.* This repetition and their slow breathing will trigger the parasympathetic nervous system, which is calm and focused.

And by doing this, they're controlling the sympathetic nervous system, controlling their cortisol levels, their stress hormones. By activating the parasympathetic nervous system they're activating the prefrontal cortex of the brain which gives them greater expansive thinking, reason and logic.

The affirmations (*I am calm, I am powerful ...*) are now linked to the feeling of ease and focus and to the chemical of oxytocin, which is the hormone of safety, connection, bliss and love. Repeating these affirmations and using this breathing technique in the future, for example during a game or event or any other pressure situation, will trigger the same emotional response from the brain and nervous system, enabling the athletes to feel exactly as they did when they rehearsed it.

Using psychological or emotional triggers is a really powerful technique that allows us to stay grounded and focused, to prepare for different potentially challenging and threatening situations before they happen and to select the emotional response that we will have in those moments. We can use visualisation, meditation, breathwork and affirmations to emotionally load a situation before it happens. Because the body uses association, once we encounter those situations for real, the body, the mind, the chemicals and the physiology of the body know it to be, or believe it to be, a memory.

This powerful emotional association is why we are always drawn towards certain people and certain situations and why we tend to avoid certain people and certain situations. Unpacking and unlocking the deeply held emotions or the emotional triggers, situations, scenarios, sounds or sites that trigger those is an incredibly powerful way to retrain and reprogram our mind, body and brain to physically, chemically, psychologically and emotionally feel and behave differently.

OUR FAMILY ENVIRONMENT

One of the greatest emotional triggers, of course, is when we go back into our family environment. The family environment is such a powerful trigger because it is the epicentre of our lives for so many of our key development years and milestones that form our identity, our emotional patterns and even shape our nervous systems.

As mentioned earlier, between the ages of zero and eight our brain is in theta brain wave, where we are literally downloading our beliefs and our emotional triggers.

Because most of us are immersed in our family, in its environment, in its dynamics during these years, we create huge emotional connections and emotional attachments to who we are, how we think, how we respond, what we're capable of, and we attach these to our family.

These can be positive or negative triggers. We've already examined how we download our belief system within the family environment from an early age. As we grow and leave the family home, we begin to develop our own set of beliefs and values. We take on new roles within the world – roles that bring us joy and form our identities – and we begin to see ourselves differently to the roles we were ascribed within the family dynamic. Returning to the family can create conflict as these roles now don't align.

When we go back to spend time with our families, we tend to start replaying the same roles in the same way, experiencing the same emotions and becoming the same person we were growing up – for example, the people-pleaser, the peacemaker, and so on. We are triggered back into our childhood state.

The gift of understanding our emotional triggers is that we can now unpack, resolve and change them. The external situation does not need to change, our family does not need to change, all we need to change is our real emotional reaction to them.

Positive emotional triggers

When I was growing up we had a busy home. There were 10 very active people living in the same house. I was a gentle child who struggled with this level of activity and I would often feel lost or overwhelmed there. Saturday mornings were different; I used to wake up early because I knew that everyone else would sleep in a little, except for my dad who would be out farming and my mum who would be up doing jobs before the chaos started. For an hour or so every Saturday morning it would be just me and my mum together in a quiet house. My mum would make me tea and toast, and I'd sit on the sofa and watch cartoons, having the whole sofa to myself and a sense of having my mum's attention and love. It was a very special time each week because I got to spend time with my mum, with whom I've always had a very close relationship. She has been my rock in my most difficult times. I can still vividly remember the quietness in the house on those mornings and the feeling of space, calm and connection. It was a sacred time for me, when it felt like everything was OK in the world.

Thirty years later and every time I go home to my parents' house I walk straight into the kitchen and make tea and toast and bring it into the sitting room; there is no better feeling, and no matter what is happening in my life it brings a sense of ease, calm and connection, a sense that I am home. It's not just in my parents' house that this happens. On occasion I will be found scurrying through the presses in our kitchen like a squirrel looking for nuts. My wife will ask, 'What are you looking for?' or she will be in another room and will hear me enquire, 'Have we any bread?' At which she will ask me what it is I am stressed about. She knows that when I am triggered to look for bread it means I am looking for a sense of calm and connection, a sense that everything is OK in the world. I think it's bread I am looking for but what I am actually looking for is something to bring me back to that sense of calm and connection I felt every Saturday morning sitting on the sofa having tea and toast.

My body, my nervous system, has now created an association, a link between eating white bread and feeling safe in the world. Bread has become my emotional trigger or my emotional stabiliser. We all have different times in our life, times of anxiety or stress or fear, when we find something that gives us a sense of calm and focus, a sense of ease, a sense of safety and security. Even though first experienced as a child, years later we can find ourselves still using these as our emotional stabilisers. It is important to know that what's happening here has very little to do with the activity itself or the foods. For example, there is no scientific evidence that bread eases anxiety or that bread is capable of calming our nervous system, yet for me it does, because it has little to do with what's in the bread and more to do with my emotional association with it and the emotional state it triggers in me. It's to do with the dopamine that our brain releases when we reward it with an activity or a substance that it believes will calm it; it's a placebo effect in action.

Dopamine is a powerful substance that gives us a sense of reward, a sense of being safe. Think of that first sip of tea or coffee in the morning or that first sip of wine from our favourite glass on a Friday night curled up on the sofa. Most people will say that as soon as they take that first sip they feel better, but we know it takes about 45 minutes for the coffee or the wine to hit our system and so that immediate sense of calm has nothing to do with what's in the cup or in the glass but rather what chemicals and emotion the activity is triggering in us and the time and place in our life the activity is taking us back to.

People with emotional eating issues refer to the food as 'comfort' or 'safety'. We can often eat to suppress an emotion, we can eat to fill an emotional void in our soul, or we can eat food or drink coffee or wine as an emotional stabiliser to trigger a feeling we crave in order to take us away from an emotion we don't want to experience. The very act of eating creates a chemical change in the brain that makes us feel safe. People who have gambling issues will often speak about their need to gamble because it gives them a 'hit', an emotional stimulation that for a very brief period gets them out of the emotional pain or the emotional numbness they feel.

We need to be careful that the emotional trigger we are using is healthy and supports the life we desire. In my own case, bread is not something that I would choose to be eating long term and is not part of my nutritional plan, so while short term in small amounts is OK, I need to look at the long term and realise that it's time to create a healthier trigger.

We must all look at our emotional stabilisers and emotional triggers and see if they are healthy in the short term and in the long term, because it is possible to change these emotional stabilisers with a little work.

Press Pause

Most of us have a coping mechanism we fall back on in times of emotional stress. It might be reaching for the tin of biscuits, a beer or a glass of wine, scrolling through our phones or even shopping. Can you think of your fallback coping mechanism to help you feel better in times of stress? Now, can you think about replacing this with something else? Instead of automatically reaching for a chocolate bar or a biscuit, would going for a run or a walk, listening to some meditative music or deep breathing help you regulate your emotions in a better way? The next time you notice yourself being triggered, try to incorporate a mindful practice to regulate your emotions and then see how this practice can become a powerful way to bring you back to a state of calm and inner peace in times of high emotion.

Creating emotional boundaries

A key factor in developing and maintaining good emotional health is establishing and protecting our emotional boundaries. Emotional boundaries involve separating our feelings from others' feelings. They help us to stop unnecessarily taking responsibility for other people's feelings and letting those feelings dictate and become more important. Healthy emotional boundaries prevent us from sacrificing our own needs in order to please others and they also stop us blaming others for our own problems. Strong boundaries protect our self-esteem and our identity as individuals with the right to make our own choices.

Emotional boundaries are our own invisible force field that we are in charge of. While most of us will know how important emotional boundaries are, many of us have a difficulty setting healthy boundaries and consistently demanding they are respected. We often fear the consequences for our relationships if we set and uphold them.

To identify when our boundaries are being crossed, we need to tune into our feelings. Good indicators are feelings of discomfort, resentment, stress, anxiety, guilt, anger and fear. The anger can be twofold: we can be angry at the person for crossing our emotional boundaries and we can be angry at ourselves for allowing our boundaries to be crossed. Guilt can also be directed at ourselves for not having the courage to demand that our emotional boundaries were respected. The fear we feel can also be twofold: we can fear the possible reaction of the other person when we demand our boundaries are respected, and we can also fear that we might actually be a person who has little to offer others if we are not constantly available to be of assistance to them. This happens when we grow up thinking our self-worth was based on how helpful we were to other people. These emotions also stem from feeling taken advantage of or not feeling appreciated. And this may not just be in relation to the present time; when someone oversteps our emotional boundaries it may well trigger deep feelings of being taken advantage of or being underappreciated or unseen as a child.

Press Pause

Do the following statements ring true for you? I can't make my own decisions; I can't ask for what I need; I can't say no; I feel criticised; I feel responsible for their feelings; I seem to take on their moods; I am often nervous, anxious or resentful around them. Maybe it's time to examine your emotional boundaries.

Unhealthy boundaries are often symptoms of a weak sense of our own identity outside of the person that helps other people. An inability to set boundaries also stems from fear – fear of abandonment or losing the relationship, fear of being judged or fear of hurting others' feelings.

Our lessons about emotional boundaries begin early in our lives, first in our families and then in our peer groups. We internalise these boundaries as a way of asserting our own needs and wants, and of taking responsibility for others' needs. How comfortable we are standing up for ourselves, expressing our emotional needs and feelings, starts very early in our development. If we grew up in a family where we never learned these healthy boundaries because of a fearful relationship with a parent, or with a sibling who we felt got all the attention, then as adults, we can find it hard to know and uphold our emotional boundaries.

Building better boundaries begins with knowing and understanding who we are and what our emotional needs are. We can begin by asking:

- Who am I?
- What am I responsible for?
- What am I not responsible for?
- Who am I responsible for?
- Who am I not responsible for?

We can also use these very simple but powerful affirmations:

- I am responsible for my behaviour, my choices, my feelings.
- I am not responsible for other people's happiness.
- I am not responsible for others' behaviours.
- I am not responsible for other people's choices.
- I am not responsible for other people's feelings.

Make a commitment to yourself to put your own identity, needs, feelings and goals first. Healthy emotional boundaries come from a commitment to letting go of: fixing other people, taking responsibility for the outcomes of others' choices, saving or rescuing others, needing to be needed, changing yourself in order to be liked, or depending on others' approval.

Press Pause

Make a list of boundaries you would like to strengthen. Write them down. Visualise yourself setting them. Assertively communicate with others what your boundaries are and when they've crossed them. Remember, this is a process. Start with a small, non-threatening boundary and experience success before taking on more challenging boundaries.

Boundaries to start with:

1. *Say no – to tasks you don't want to do or don't have time to do.*
2. *Say yes – to help.*
3. *Say thank you with no apology, regret or shame.*
4. *Ask for help.*
5. *Delegate tasks.*
6. *Protect your time – don't overcommit.*
7. *Ask for space – we all need our own time.*
8. *Speak up if you feel uncomfortable with how someone is treating you or that your needs are being infringed upon.*
9. *Honour what is important to you by choosing to put yourself first.*
10. *Drop the guilt and responsibility for others.*
11. *Share personal information gradually and in a mutual way (give and take).*

Healthy boundaries are a sign of good emotional health, of self-respect and strength. If we teach people how to treat us, set high standards for those we surround ourselves with, expect to be treated in the same loving way we treat them, we will soon find ourselves surrounded by those who respect us, care about our needs and our feelings and who treat us with kindness.

Releasing the emotions that aren't serving us

How heavy something feels (be it physical, emotional or psychological) is defined by three things:

1. The weight of the thing itself
2. The length of time we carry it
3. Our resistance to it

Emotions that we hold for a short time have far less ability to have a lasting negative impact on our happiness and our health, but the same emotions held for a sustained or prolonged period can have a far more negative impact. The longer we hold onto a negative emotion, the longer it takes for us to come back out of our stress mode. The length of time we spend in an emotion is as important as the emotion itself. There is a beautiful Buddhist story that gives a perfect example of how we often hold onto emotions long after it is necessary.

LESSONS FROM AN OLD MONK

A old monk and a junior monk were travelling together. At one point, they came to a river with a strong current. As the monks were preparing to cross the river, they saw a woman also attempting to cross. She asked if they could help her cross to the other side. The two monks glanced at one another because they had taken vows not to touch a woman. Then, without a word, the older monk picked up the woman, carried her across the river, placed her on the other side and carried on his journey. The younger monk couldn't believe what had just happened. After rejoining his companion he

---

was speechless, and an hour passed without a word between them. Two more hours passed, then three, until finally the younger monk couldn't contain himself any longer. 'As monks,' he said, 'we are not permitted to touch a woman – how could you then carry that woman on your shoulders?' The older monk looked at him and replied, 'Brother, I set her down on the other side of the river, why are you still carrying her?'

If we continue to carry around past hurts, holding onto resentments, then the only person we are really hurting is ourselves. We all go through times in our lives when other people say things or behave in a way that is hurtful towards us. We can choose to ruminate over the past but ultimately this prevents us from moving through periods of stress and high emotion and keeps us locked in fight-or-flight mode. When we hold onto emotions for prolonged periods of time they will weigh us down, take away our inner peace and eventually create physical illness.

Emotions are short-lived emotional charges and left to themselves they quickly expire. In order to continue, they need someone to keep giving them a new charge; they need us to stay committed to that emotion and to maintaining that emotion and so they hijack our thoughts and our awareness. The only person who can generate or perpetuate an emotion in me is me, and so – as mentioned earlier – we need to stop poking the bear. If the bear keeps biting us, we need to stop poking it. If the emotion is hurting, we must stop poking it.

We must be aware and accept that emotions cannot continue unless there is something or someone perpetuating them. We can be in the same emotion all morning, all afternoon, all day, all week and very often we don't question who or what is perpetuating it.

One of the ways we can regulate our emotions is to become aware of the inner narrative that we are allowing to run inside our minds and the words we are choosing. We need to ask ourselves if this inner narrative is giving us access to a new and more helpful emotion or keeping us trapped in unhelpful emotions. When we consciously start to change this inner narrative, we disrupt the narrative, and the more we change the direction of the narrative the more we change the direction and nature of the emotion.

Press Pause

Try to think of someone who has hurt you in the past. How long did you carry that hurt? Are you still carrying it? How much energy are you giving it? How heavy is this weighing on you? Is it time to lay down your hurt and anger by the side of the lake? In order to lay it down, try a simple practical exercise like writing down what which you wish to release. Then create a ritual or ceremony whereby you tear up or burn what you have written and you release it back into the universe, letting it go. Send love, release bitterness and allow peace to come back into your heart.

PERMISSION TO BE HAPPY

We must give ourselves permission to be happy, permission to be healthy and permission to be successful. This will at times mean that we have to be willing to step freely out of and away from the need to please others, to be the same as others, to share the same beliefs as others and engage in the same life choices as others, even if these others are our family. It will at times mean we need to surrender our fear of being the success we dream of and surrender the need to downplay ourselves and our success so that we don't upset others. In her bestselling book *A Return to Love* (1992), Marianne Williamson spoke about how we should not shrink ourselves or play small in the world. Giving ourselves permission to be happy, to be successful and to be free is also about giving others permission to be free from our expectations.

We must be careful not to want more happiness or success for others than they want for themselves or are willing to commit to. If we don't set ourselves free to live and to shine on our own terms we will end up either dragging others into our expectations and limits or dragging ourselves back into theirs. We can of course support, guide and assist others but we can never drag someone to a level of happiness or success that they are not willing to give themselves.

Many people are committed to their own limitations and to trying to reinforce and prove to themselves that their limitations are real and unavoidable, and this commitment means they can never move beyond them. The question we need to ask ourselves is: are we willing to move beyond our limitations without fear and without judgement of self or others? We are all on our own journey and it's important we allow others to be on theirs.

Playing small, denying our inner dreams and ambitions, is not just cheating ourselves: it's cheating others and the universe out of the greatness we were born with and the greatness we were born to be. We have an incredible message and we are born to share our message with the whole world; by denying ourselves and downplaying our own greatness we are cheating the universe out of an incredible gift. It is not selfish to leave a tribe so that we can shine – in fact, it is selfish to stay within that tribe and allow them to dim our light.

Emotional regulation

By now, we will hopefully have a better understanding of how we carry our unconscious emotions, how they impact our everyday emotions, where they come from and how we can observe and dissolve them by slowing down and leaning into the discomfort. Below, we will examine how we can also observe and change our emotional reactions in a practical way.

The shorter our emotional refractory period, the less we suffer

Our emotional refractory phase is the time it takes us to move out of one emotional state into another. If we can learn how to shorten this refractory period, we can better our emotional health.

Lessons from a gazelle

There is an expression attributed to Roger Bannister, the first man to run a mile under four minutes, about the relationship between a gazelle and a lion.

Every day in Africa a gazelle wakes up. It knows it must run faster than the fastest lion or it will be killed. Every morning a lion wakes up. It knows that it must outrun the slowest gazelle or it will starve to death.

To survive, the gazelle must be in *consistent* alert to a potential threat, or else it will become dinner for a hungry lion. I deliberately use the word consistent because it is important to distinguish between consistent and constant. The gazelle is very consistent in its alertness and defensive reactions in the face of threat but this state of alert isn't constant. The incredible thing about gazelles is that they can be totally at ease and relaxed until the moment of attack and then they have an amazing ability to switch on their fight-or-flight mode to fight or flee from the lion. They have an equally impressive ability to switch off their fight-or-flight response the moment the attack is over. After one of the herd has been caught by the lion, the other gazelles, knowing the lion now has enough to eat, can quickly return to a place of calm, even while still in the midst of the lions. This is because they know that the source of attack and the danger is over, for now. This ability to switch on and off their stress response can be measured by examining their chemistry, biology and actions.

What is important to note is that they only turn on their stress response when there is an actual threat – unlike us humans, who view actual threats and perceived threats in the same way.

We too have the amazing ability to switch on our stress, fight-or-flight response but we can also forget how to switch it off once the threat has passed. In fact, as we have seen through my flight-turbulence analogy earlier, we don't even need a real threat to switch on our chemical and biological stress response. The threat can be real, remembered from the past or even imagined. The brain, which is an active threat-detection system, will never wait to see if the threat is real. The moment we think about a threat, we switch on our fight-or-flight mode and activate our sympathetic nervous system, and if we live in a constant state of perceived threat it can be difficult to switch this mode off, meaning that we live in a general state of fight or flight.

Developing our emotional refractory phase, our inner gazelle

As we begin to tune in more to our observer self, to acknowledge our unconscious emotions and our emotional reactions, we can begin to reduce our emotional refractory period. So when we find ourselves reacting to external stimuli, our new sense of awareness can allow us to pause, let the emotion sit, challenge that emotion, ask ourselves where it is coming from and eventually allow that emotion to pass. As we tap into our observer self more and more, we can recognise the times where we are operating from the sympathetic nervous system and we can move out of this.

How to shorten our emotional refractory period

The quickest way to become more consciously aware of our emotions and to change them is to use a multidisciplinary approach that shifts and changes our biology, our neurocircuitry, our chemistry and our frequency.

When we experience moments of high emotion or know that we are entering into a situation that will be emotionally triggering, there are various practices that can help with changing our emotional responses.

Learning how to recognise our unconscious emotions and when and how to set them down is vital to reducing our refractory periods. The more we can recognise where an emotion comes from, the sooner we can move through it and return to a state of rest and digest.

The multidimensional approach to emotional regulation

As we have explored, emotions have a physical and chemical dimension so in order to help us regulate our emotions, we must engage in activities that regulate our biology, our chemistry and our physiology. We have all heard the term exorcism, which usually applies to removing a ghost-like entity. A ghost is a non-physical energy being. Whether ghosts exist or not, this gives us a new way of thinking about exercise. Maybe exercise, like an exorcism, is a powerful way of

> 'The more we can recognise where an emotion comes from, the sooner we can move through it and return to a state of rest and digest.'

removing negative energy and is as much to do with changing negative energy as building the body.

The vagus nerve

There is a constant feedback loop between our body and mind, known as the mind–body connection. A critical component of the mind–body connection is the vagus nerve, which is an integral part of our autonomic nervous system. This part of the nervous system controls the things our body does without our conscious input, such as breathing, digestion, sweating, heart rate, taste, speech, skin sensations, muscle sensations, immune response, respiratory rate, blood pressure, mucus production, saliva production, frequency of urination and mood.

Specifically, the vagus nerve is part of the parasympathetic nervous system, which calms our body after we've been in a stressful situation. It carries signals from our brain to other parts of our body, such as our heart or intestines, to initiate this process.

The vagus (vagal) nerve is also known as the tenth cranial nerve or cranial nerve X. It starts in our medulla oblongata, a part of the brain that connects to the spinal cord, and splits off into many branches that extend down through our neck to our vital abdominal organs. This long nerve makes up three-quarters of the nerve tissue in our parasympathetic nervous system. In fact, the vagus nerve is the longest of any of the 12 cranial nerves.

What does the vagus nerve do?

The vagus nerve helps our body exit its fight-or-flight mode. It sends information from the gut to the brain, which is linked to dealing with stress, anxiety and fear – hence the saying 'gut feeling'. These signals help us to recover from stressful situations. Our vagus nerve helps disengage our sympathetic nervous system. Vagus nerve stimulation (VNS) increases parasympathetic nervous system activity, counterbalancing fight-or-flight stress responses. The vagus nerve can be toned and strengthened like a muscle. We can stimulate and strengthen our vagus nerve and vagal tone using very simple yet powerful techniques.

Cold immersion

Research shows that when our body adjusts to cold, our fight-or-flight (sympathetic) system declines and our rest-and-digest (parasympathetic) system increases – and this is mediated by the vagus nerve. Any kind of acute cold exposure will increase vagus nerve activation.

Gargling

A simple remedy for an under-stimulated vagus nerve is to gargle water. Gargling actually stimulates the muscles of the palate which are fired by the vagus nerve.

Singing and chanting

Humming, mantra chanting, hymn singing and upbeat energetic singing all increase heart rate variability (HRV) in slightly different ways. Essentially, singing is like initiating a vagal pump, sending out relaxing waves. Singing at the top of our lungs works the muscles in the back of the throat to activate the vagus. When we sing in unison, it also increases HRV and vagus function.

Massage

We can stimulate our vagus nerve by massaging our feet and our neck along the carotid sinus, located along the carotid arteries on either side of our neck. A pressure massage can also activate the vagus nerve.

Laughter

Happiness and laughter are natural immune boosters. Laughter also stimulates the vagus nerve. Research shows that laughter increases HRV in a group environment.

Yoga and tai chi

Both increase vagus nerve activity and our parasympathetic system in general. Studies have shown that yoga increases GABA, a calming neurotransmitter in our brain. Researchers believe it does this by 'stimulating vagal afferents (fibres)', which increase activity in the parasympathetic nervous system. This is especially helpful for those who struggle with anxiety or depression. Tai chi can also 'enhance vagal modulation'.

Positive social relationships

There is amazing evidence that healthy and positive social relationships actually have an important impact on our vagus nerve. Positive connections with others lead to an improvement in vagal function, as seen in heart rate variability.

Breathing deeply and slowly

Our heart and neck contain neurons that have receptors called baroreceptors, which detect blood pressure and transmit the neuronal signal to our brain. This activates our vagus nerve that connects to our heart to lower blood pressure and heart rate. Slow breathing, with a roughly equal amount of time breathing in and out, increases the sensitivity of baroreceptors and vagal activation. Breathing around five to six breaths per minute, for the average adult, can be very helpful.

Exercise

Exercise increases our brain's growth hormone, supports our brain's mitochondria, and helps reverse cognitive decline. But it has also been shown to stimulate the vagus nerve, which leads to beneficial brain and mental health effects. Mild exercise also stimulates gut flow, which is mediated by the vagus nerve.

Relaxation

Allowing the mind to rest in the present moment or being engaged in an activity we love, one that allows time and the outside world to disappear and enables us to become truly present in those moments, has an amazing ability to regulate our nervous system and our vagus nerve.

Meditation

Meditation is a term given to a number of practices that involve focusing or clearing one's mind using a combination of mental and physical techniques, and many of the practices also encompass various breathing techniques. Every type of meditation involves methods to enhance attention, emotional awareness, kindness, compassion, sympathetic joy and mental calmness even in difficult situations. Meditation can be a still practice or it can be an active and dynamic practice involving movement.

Depending on the type of meditation we choose, it can be practised to help us relax, reduce anxiety and stress, and gain greater awareness and insights into our inner stories and emotions.

During meditation, self-awareness develops by acknowledging and accepting our internal thoughts and feelings that arise throughout the practice without judgement, and it allows us to explore not just these thoughts and feelings but their root cause and whether they are real or simply imagined. The ability to quieten the thinking brain that is always commenting and reacting to various stimuli, and instead activate our observer self that can be aware of the presence of various stimuli, external or internal, without the need to react, attach or comment on them, is one of the greatest gifts of meditation.

Meditation is not about getting distracted; although we may become distracted a number of times, meditation increases our ability to return to a state of presence, releasing us from the distraction and allowing us to return to a single point of focus. This single point of focus can be our breath, our mantra or an inner image we are creating, or it can simply be where we become beautifully aware that there is a part of us that is outside our thoughts, outside our stories, outside our excuses, outside our emotions and outside our bodies. The activation and connection to this higher-awareness self gives us a powerful sense of connection and of being at one with everything. The word zen simply means 'oneness'.

Meditation is scientifically proven to create changes in our brain chemistry which allow us to proactively replace the stress chemicals such as cortisol with feel-good chemicals such as dopamine and oxytocin, which results in slowing down thoughts, improving concentration, reducing fear, anxiety and stress and increasing emotional feelings of connection, love, joy and gratitude.

Neuroscience also indicates that meditation tends to lead to an increase in the production of theta and alpha waves, which are the brain wave frequencies associated with enhanced learning abilities and overall mental well-being.

Daily mindful meditation practice has been shown to produce measurable changes in brain regions associated with memory, sense of self, empathy and stress.

Meditation activates the parasympathetic nervous system, which is our rest-and-repair system, and it downregulates the sympathetic nervous system, which is our threat-based survival system. And in doing this it allows the body and our various physiological systems – including our immune system – to repair.

Breathing

We can reset our nervous system naturally by using deep-breathing techniques. Breathing in fully, then exhaling fully, allowing the exhale to be longer than the inhale, has been shown to return the autonomic nervous system from an over-activated sympathetic state to a more balanced parasympathetic state. A deep sigh is our body-brain's natural way to release tension and reset our nervous system.

Box breathing, diaphragmatic breathing and alternate nostril breathing are all great ways to invite calm during a state of panic. The human lungs have a capacity of four litres approximately yet most adults when tested are using only half a litre of this capacity. We are breathing too shallowly and this switches on our fight-or-flight response. We are meant to take between four and eight breaths per minute, but when tested most adults are taking twenty or more breaths per minute. This fast-breathing rate again sends a signal to the brain that a threat is either present or imminently present and so our sympathetic fight-or-flight response is switched on. Patrick McKeown, author of *The Oxygen Advantage*, has done some great research on the impact and power of specific breathing techniques to enhance our health, performance and well-being.

Vitamins

Our vitamin level plays an important role in the function and regulation of our nervous system. Neurotropic B vitamins are crucially important as coenzymes in the nervous system. Particularly vitamin B1 (thiamine), B6 (pyridoxine) and B12 (cobalamin) contribute essentially to the maintenance of a healthy nervous system.

Retrain our neural pathways by doing things differently

Another simple but powerful way of changing our subconscious beliefs is to do things differently. Unconscious beliefs can be referred to as a redundant set of habits and behaviours that are predictable and not necessarily even relevant. Up to 90 per cent of our daily habits are unconscious. The things we buy, the food we eat, the words we use, the actions we take when we first wake in the morning become so ingrained, so familiar, that we are no longer even aware that we're doing them.

Press Pause

Tomorrow morning when you wake up, instead of reaching for your phone to check the news, switch on a guided meditation, or get out of bed and do 15 minutes of stretching. Try to do this for one full week and see if you feel any differently.

When we begin to do things differently, for example answering the phone with our opposite hand, standing on one foot while brushing our teeth, it fires the brain out of unconscious programs and into conscious awareness. The more we do things differently, the more we fire and wire new neurons and create new neurological pathways. These pathways fire a new signal into our nervous system, to which our body responds and begins to crave our new behaviours. After a little time our brains add in dopamine, the powerful reward chemical, to affirm these new behaviours, which means we are becoming chemically wired to them. Dopamine is released by the brain every time we fulfil an expected behaviour or thought pattern. Our dopamine attachment to certain habits and situations keeps us locked in a state of constantly fulfilling our deepest beliefs. This is why when we begin to think and/or act differently we begin to feel uneasiness. The brain initially recognises that it is not going to get its hit of dopamine because we are no longer fulfilling old beliefs and behaviours, and not only does it start to crave the dopamine but it actually produces cortisol, our stress hormone, to try and derail us from the new behaviour and thinking pattern.

In order to change our deepest beliefs we must be willing to feel stressful and uneasy for the initial phase and break free from the chemical addiction to old beliefs and habits while forging new positive pathways.

Using these tools in daily life

The above are tools we can use to regulate our emotional responses in specific situations, and we can practise them regularly so that we are more in control of our emotions and our emotional responses. It can also be useful to adopt some or all of these in our daily routine so that we begin to feel more balanced and more aware of our emotional health.

Try any of these individual techniques such as breathing, meditation or movement when you know you are entering into a situation or are in a situation of heightened emotion – like before a presentation, in a difficult conversation or if you experience social anxiety. See how the awareness allows you to become more conscious of where your emotional reaction is coming from and how you can change this when you become more aware of it.

Creating a routine

My morning routine is a mix of energising my body through movement – such as boxing or running – and chanting, yoga and breathwork to stimulate and regulate my central nervous system. We might think of our emotions as non-material, non-physical or as happening only in our mind, but as we now know, emotions are also very physical. This is why exercise and movement are so important in regulating our emotional states. To change a powerful emotion we must change not just our thinking but also our biology, our chemistry and our physiology. This is why physical activities, like exercise, cold-water immersion, dancing, and so on, are an important way to rebalance our central nervous system and bring it from a state of disregulation to a place of regulation.

Once the body and nervous system are moving and releasing, I then build in visualisation to activate the firing of important and positive brain neurons. When we deliberately start to fire thoughts about what we can control and what we are grateful for, and when we start to think about the things we want and not the things we fear, our brain sends new electrical signals into the nervous system, electrical signals that are no longer associated with threat and fear, where only bad things happen, but are instead associated with control and opportunity. Once we switch our thinking from threat-based to opportunity-based we are sending completely different signals into our body and nervous system and we quickly begin to feel safer, more grounded and more at ease in our body. This in turn sends a powerful signal back to the brain and now the body and brain are working together to perpetuate these new feelings and emotions of control, safety and empowerment.

In an ever-changing, unpredictable and uncertain world, multidimensional morning routines are key. They are a really important way of changing and regulating our emotional state and in doing so regulating our nervous system, our immune system, our hormonal system and our chemistry. Along with the above-mentioned routines, there are also other important ways we can change emotions and better regulate our inner emotional state.

WEEKLY MORNING ROUTINE

Below is a sample weekly routine that I follow to try to keep myself balanced and regulated.

Monday: 06:30
5k run, stretch, followed by a sea swim

Tuesday: 06:30
45 mins circuit and resistance training, 15 mins meditation, 15 mins journaling, followed by a cold shower or sea swim

Wednesday: 06:30
45 mins yoga and breathwork, 15 mins meditation, followed by a cold shower

Thursday: 06:30
7— 10k run, followed by a sea swim
Friday: 06:30
5k run, sauna, dip in an ice bath

I also like to include three boxing sessions per week, fifteen minutes of positive affirmations per day and three longer meditations during the week.

Press Pause

Create a little weekly map or schedule for yourself that will include and incorporate some or all of the above spread throughout the week. Why not rotate and try new things each day for a week? See what resonates with you and see how you can challenge yourself to use different practices and techniques to activate your vagus nerve and bring you home to a more balanced, unified and coherent state.

I hope this section has shown you that emotions are not our enemy, they are not here to be destructive, but they are here to be disruptive. We are sent vital messages at times when we need a disruption to our normal actions, thinking and habits and when we need a disruption and redirection in our lives. When we choose not to run from them, not to hide from them and not to suppress them and instead choose to feel them, heal them and release them we realise not just the power of emotions but the power we have over our emotions.

MEDITATION FOR REMOVING EMOTIONAL BLOCKS

Relax your body and find a comfortable position. Take a deep breath, filling your lungs with fresh air, and slowly exhale, releasing any tension or stress.

Now, visualise yourself standing in a calming space, surrounded by gentle, soothing energy. Feel its warmth and positive vibrations embracing you.

With each breath you take, imagine this healing energy flowing into your body, travelling from the top of your head all the way down to the tips of your toes. Allow it to dissolve any emotional blocks or barriers that you may be carrying within you.

As you exhale, release these emotional blocks with intention, letting go of any negative emotions or limiting beliefs that no longer serve you. Visualise them leaving your body as dark clouds dissipating into the air. Feel a sense of relief and lightness.

Continue breathing deeply, focusing on the rhythm of your breath. With each inhale, imagine yourself drawing in fresh energy and rejuvenation. With each exhale, imagine releasing any remaining emotional blocks, allowing them to be transformed and replaced with positivity.

Stay in this state of relaxation and mindfulness for a few moments, basking in the newfound sense of freedom and emotional release. When you are ready, slowly open your eyes and carry this feeling of emotional liberation with you throughout your day.

Remember, you have the power to remove emotional blocks and create a life filled with joy and fulfilment. Embrace this power and allow yourself to fully experience the freedom that comes with letting go.

Press Pause

Journaling exercise for emotional awareness

Find a quiet and comfortable space where you can focus on your thoughts and emotions without distractions. Grab a pen and a journal or a blank sheet of paper.

Start by taking a few deep breaths to centre yourself. Close your eyes and bring your attention inward. Scan your body and notice any physical sensations or tension that you may be holding onto. Take note of these sensations without judgement.

Now, begin writing freely about your current emotional state. Let your thoughts flow onto the page without any filters or restrictions. Explore how you're feeling and what may have triggered or contributed to those emotions. Allow yourself to be completely honest and vulnerable in your writing.

As you journal, reflect on the following prompts to further deepen your emotional awareness:

1. *How does this emotion feel in my body? Are there any specific areas where I feel it the most?*
2. *Can I identify any thoughts or beliefs that may be fuelling these emotions? Are these thoughts helpful or harmful to my overall well-being?*
3. *Are there any recurring patterns or themes in my emotions? Do I tend to feel this way in certain situations or with certain people?*
4. *What is the underlying need or desire behind these emotions? Is there something I can do to fulfil this need or address this desire?*
5. *How can I practise self-compassion and self-care in response to these emotions? What actions or practices would support my emotional well-being?*

Continue writing for as long as you feel necessary. Once you have finished, take a moment to reflect on what you have written. Notice any insights, patterns or revelations that arose as you explored your emotions on paper.

Remember, this journaling exercise is a tool for self-reflection and emotional awareness. Be kind and patient with yourself as you navigate your emotions, and allow this process to guide you towards greater understanding and growth.

SUMMARY

- Letting go of the harmful beliefs that are having an impact on our lives and how to do this
- Learning how to reprime our reticular activating system to manage our emotions
- The importance of slowing down to meet our unconscious emotional wounds – yin yoga
- The emotional stabilisers preventing us from changing
- Understanding emotional triggers – how they work and how we can learn to create new, positive ones
- Emotional boundaries and their importance
- Releasing the emotions that aren't serving us
- Emotional regulation – understanding it and the multidimensional approach

4

The Freedom:
A New Way of Living

Earlier in the book we explored the powerful and transformative effect of awakening our observer self. We saw how this higher level of awareness is constant while our thinking and emotional self is temporary. But the question is what are the practices that allow us to maintain this deeper level of perspective, this calmness, this fearlessness and this ability to live beyond the temporary and beyond emotion?

Living with emotional freedom

It was March 2020, we were just about to have our first baby, our business, after years of trying to get it off the ground, years of living with little or no financial return, was beginning to take off. We had invested a lot into bringing our message into more countries and had taken a big chance by booking venues so that we could host seminars over the next 12 months in a number of different places abroad. We had employed more people to help the business grow and we had both great opportunities and a great responsibility to make it work, not just for ourselves and the risks we were taking but also for the people who had left good jobs to come and work for us.

We had just opened our first gym after a major financial spend kitting it out, and we were so excited to have our own physical space where we could host our clients. Our business was going well, it was an in-person business (at that point we had never done an online talk and neither was it in our plans); we were fully committed to live, in-person shows. At the same time, we had just moved into a house where we had committed to a two-year rental contract. It was finely balanced but, if everything stayed the same, we would be fine. We had done a lot of planning, and all the plans were saying that everything would work well. We believed we had a predictable 18 months ahead.

But you know what they say about the best-laid plans! There is an expression that says, 'If you want to make the universe laugh, tell it your plans and tell it that you are in control.' The moment the ego takes over and you think that you are the one in control, you'd better stand back and get ready for an adventure. The universe was about to bring us on an incredible adventure and give us one of the greatest lessons of our lives.

One afternoon, as I sat down for dinner, I went to turn off the TV, and as I did so a newsflash appeared about a thing called Covid. And at that moment all our carefully made plans became redundant.

In the space of a week Covid and the response to it was in full swing: all our events for the considerable future were cancelled, our deposits were lost, our diaries emptied, our gym was closed, we were now looking at a business with zero income. We had wages to pay, rent to pay, a new baby on the way, no family anywhere near us as we live on the opposite side of the country and we were not allowed to travel. So we were dealing with all this without even a family member to share a cup of tea with.

The world seemed to be plunged into a frenzy of fear and uncertainty. Life had changed so dramatically in a few days and now it was time for calm heads, calm minds and to really see if freedom is still possible despite physical restrictions. With our new baby on the way and my wife with no support around her only me, it was time I let go of fear, it was time I let go of limitation, and instead of focusing on what I didn't have and what I couldn't do, it was time to focus on what I did have and what I could do: it was time to put aside restriction and go after liberation.

If this had happened to me a few years before I am not sure how I would have coped, but now there was a certainty, a calmness and a clarity within me that was unstoppable. I remember one morning, after doing one of my usual morning routines, coming into the kitchen to jump on a Zoom call with my team at work. I could see that they were nervous about everything that was happening, worried about their loved ones, worried about themselves and worried about their jobs. I sat down with a cup of tea. I was in a zone of manifestation, and I remember telling the team that this was going to be an incredible year, a year of incredible challenge and incredible learning and a year when our business, Soul Space, would stand up for what we believed in: truth, human connection, kindness, compassion, freedom, empowerment and service.

They looked at me as if I had 10 heads, but quickly I knew that they could see in me what I could feel – clarity, certainty and trust. They knew I was plugged into something bigger than me and empowered by a mission bigger than me.

Then of course they asked the obvious question: 'How are we going to do that?'

'I don't know,' I answered, 'but if we open our minds, the universe will tell us. We will focus on one day at a time, we will commit to being of service to others and in a time of fear and segregation we will commit to being a voice of calm and connection. Sometimes, you don't need to see the end – sometimes you can just about see the first step and that first step is all you really need. Once you take that step, with a calm heart and an open mind, the next step somehow always appears. So let's take the first step and see where it leads us.'

A year later, we had a beautiful one-year-old boy. We had

'Sometimes you don't know how strong you are until strong is the only option.'

created a thriving online business, I had written a best-selling book, we had an incredible online community, all of which would never have happened if we were not put into that situation. Sometimes you don't know how strong you are until strong is the only option.

In times of darkness, light the little light you have and welcome the weary traveller

I have been asked so many times how we did it. Some of it was luck, lots of it was surrounding myself with incredible people and more of it came down to my ability to stay focused on my *why*, to remind myself of the mission statement we use every single day in our business: *In times of darkness, light the little light you have and welcome the weary traveller.*

A passionate devotion to serving others is one of the greatest and most empowering reinforcers there is. There is something incredibly empowering when you begin to see life through the lens of service and I decided that instead of getting caught up in my own fears and my own needs I would focus on the needs of others. I would use this as a time where, no matter how small the impact I could have, I would attempt to be a positive force every single day; from the words I used to the conversations I had, every interaction would be infused with a kind, positive and uplifting energy. When we live with and are motivated by the desire to empower other people, to be of service, to learn and to be an expression of truth, joy and peace, we are grounded in service, joy and peace and in a state of being where the process and the journey becomes as important as the outcome.

Of course to be of service to others we must enable ourselves to have that level of energy and we must work hard to ensure that our own mindset and energy is where we need it to be.

Separate the work from the tasks

I decided to divide everything into two categories: (1) the work; (2) the tasks.

The tasks were the things I had to do every day, from housework, to preparing for our new baby, to setting up a new business. The work, the real work, was the things I needed to do to get myself right before I started on the tasks. For me it has always been more important to focus on the way in which we bring ourselves to any task than the task itself. If we approach any task, no matter how big or small, in the right mindset, with perspective, with positivity, with energy and with ease, then the task becomes a little bit easier. If, on the other hand, we bring ourselves to a task in the wrong frame of mind, where we do not have the right energy, or focus, or perspective, if we do not bring a sense of ease into the task then the task cannot be easy.

The very first commitment I made was that I would consistently focus on doing the daily work to ensure that as the challenges – the tasks – arrived over the next few months, I would bring the right mindset, the right energy, the right focus and that I would approach the tasks in an empowered manner. There was so much that we could not control, and if I allowed my energy, my attention and my awareness to be consumed by that, I would be allowing myself to be disempowered. And so I focused only on the things I could control; I focused on what I had and not what I didn't have, on where my freedom was and not where my limitation was.

Before we tackle any external task we must first be willing to do the internal work. Now was a time to look deep inside, to identify, name and live my values, and I created a set of principles by which I would now live and would no longer live by emotion. When we live by emotion, when we allow our emotions to decide our actions, then our actions will be temporary and in a state of flux just like our emotions. When we decide to live by principles, these are permanent and steadfast and independent of emotions.

Behind each of these principles I created a set of practices that allowed me to achieve the principle. My daily practices included: morning sunrise exercise, meditation, journaling, cold-water immersion, either through a cold shower (last two minutes cold), ice bath or sea swim.

In the evening my night-time routines for enhanced sleep included: (1) turning my phone off two hours before going to bed; the white light of the phone activates the brain and the brain thinks it's daytime so doesn't produce melatonin, which is the hormone we need for sleep – a warm bath or a warm shower before bed can help produce melatonin; (2) journaling to get all the thoughts from the day out of my head; (3) yoga nidra or a simple meditation to calm the nervous system; (4) not eating or drinking anything that stimulates me.

Every day is a lifetime and every lifetime is a day

Every single morning, without fail, whether I felt like it or not, I committed to my morning routines at the same time as when I had been working. I continued to get up every day at 5.30 a.m. and meet the dawn with a renewed focus and determination.

With no work to go to I could easily have had a lie-in, but this was not a time to lie down, it was a time to stand up. I turned our sitting room into a home gym. I stopped watching TV – I didn't need any more fear being pumped into my home. I created a meditation space in my attic where I committed to making my meditation practice better and more consistent than ever. I offered free online meditations for anyone who wanted to try them. I focused on being of service to others. The moment we remind ourselves that one of the best ways to be happy is to help others be happy is the moment we realise the emotional power of service. I might only have a small bit to contribute but, whatever I could, I gave it all with a full heart. The more I committed to these inner practices, the more I was able to achieve the principles, and the more I focused on principles and practices, the less my emotions had a say in my life.

Life doesn't have to get easier, our challenges don't have to get smaller, but we can always get stronger

Every morning during my morning routine I reminded myself that life doesn't have to get easier; our challenges don't have to get smaller, but we can always get stronger. I repeated this mantra over and over every single morning. Once I stopped waiting for life to get easier and the challenges to get smaller,

I started to focus on making myself stronger, calmer, more grateful; and the less I focused on physical restriction, the more I focused on mental and emotional liberation. I realised that life does not have to be easy but that I could be strong, I could be fearless, I could be kind, I could pursue joy and love and no-one could take that away from me.

The pillars of emotional freedom

The principles I'd decided to live by during Covid became my pillars of emotional freedom which I go into in more detail in the final section of this book. Over the years, truly living these pillars has been my greatest challenge and my greatest freedom. They have enabled me to come to a whole new understanding of the universe, of awareness and of myself; they have allowed me to live a life where I am guided, directed and motivated by my principles and not my emotions.

They are not always easy to live but they are absolutely worth the challenge. They have empowered me with a new ability to navigate the ups and downs and the uncertainties of life with greater ease, awareness, curiosity, confidence, joy and fearlessness. These principles have become my inner compass and when faced with my biggest decisions they have allowed me to not be distracted by fear or anxiety, not be distracted by other people or other people's opinions, but instead stay focused on my own power, stay true to my own dreams and step bravely into the unknown, somehow knowing that everything will work out in a way that makes perfect sense. They are the principles that enable me to accept the things that happen unexpectedly or in ways that I didn't want or predict and not get overwhelmed by them but instead successfully navigate my way through them, enabling me to rise and thrive in challenge and change. I work on these pillars of emotional freedom all the time to help me stay emotionally connected to what is important and to emotionally release myself from all that no longer serves me.

All of these pillars are habits. We can choose to develop the habit of comparison or the habit of non-comparison, the habit of attachment or non-attachment, of striving or non-striving, of forgiving or non-forgiving, of gratitude or non-gratitude, of surrender or non-surrender. What I know for sure is that once we develop the habit, we are likely to perpetuate it over and over regardless of our external world, and it is these internal emotional habits, and not our external situations, that are actually the predictor of how happy we will be. These are the habits of emotional freedom and the habits of happiness and for me these are the greatest habits there are.

Here are my pillars of emotional freedom:
1. Non-resistance
2. Non-judgement
3. Non-attachment
4. Non-striving
5. Forgiveness
6. Non-comparison
7. Trust
8. Gratitude
9. The emotional power of why
10. Surrender

1. Non-resistance

Very often the biggest cause of our suffering is not actually the external event but our anticipation, our expectation, our internal experience and our reaction to the external event. Earlier in this book I said that how heavy something feels is defined by three things:

1. The weight of the thing itself
2. The length of time we carry it
3. Our resistance to it

You will remember that the story of the monks crossing the river was about how long we carry something, so here I want to talk about how our resistance to something is very often what makes a load too heavy to carry and the obstacle too large for us to overcome.

Resistance is like a person standing on a beach fighting a tide, trying to push it back out because he is not ready for it. The tide is guided and directed by a force that is far more powerful than we are. If we fight it or resist it, we will simply end up depleted, frustrated and disempowered. When we can accept the things that are outside of our control, outside of what we expected, we can attach our energy and focus onto the things we can control. Non-resistance means that we can accept what is, without judgement. This allows us to flow more easily with life and to live more in an inner state of ease and grace.

Non-resistance is not about rolling over and accepting that there is nothing we can do to change the things we don't want.

It is about facing the things we don't want with kindness, love and empowered choice in order to change them from how they are to how we want them to be.

Empowered acceptance

Very often the way to decrease the weight of a load or to decrease the size of a challenge is to stop resisting it. Acceptance is the first part of non-resistance, but not in the sense that we roll over in a state of victimhood. Empowered acceptance is about accepting things as they are in that moment, so that we don't waste an ounce of energy on what we don't want. Instead, we make an immediate and informed decision to put our awareness, attention and energy into what we do want. Resisting something, giving out about, it will do absolutely nothing except deplete our energy, our mindset and our motivation. Empowered acceptance is not about fighting the old, it is about building the new.

Press Pause

- *Where in your life are you resisting something that you can't control?*
- *Where in your life are you wishing things were different instead of accepting them as they are?*
- *Think of an example of where your expectation or anticipation of something is making the thing harder than it actually is.*

- *What would it take for you to accept things as they are?*
- *What is the cost to you and to others of your resistance?*
- *What is the thing that you can control?*
- *What is the thing that you can focus on that would give you a sense of empowerment back?*
- *What would taking your power back look like?*
- *What would taking your power back sound like?*
- *Are your inner stories right now ones of self-empowerment or disempowerment?*
- *What would a better story sound like?*
- *What would an empowered and emotionally free person think and do if they were in your situation?*
- *Who are you waiting for to give you a sense of empowerment?*

---

2. Non-judgement

A number of years ago I was getting some building work done in my house. At the time, it looked like the builder had done a great job. But very shortly after the work was completed, some issues began to appear. Initially, I wasn't too upset about this because the issues weren't anything major and I believed that the builder would come back and put them right.

However, I soon realised that it might not be as simple as I expected. The builder wasn't answering my calls, and the more I called, the more frustrated I became. When I couldn't get hold of the builder, I asked friends what they thought I should do and of course they all had different opinions. The dominant opinion was 'Oh, they've got the money and now they are gone, they couldn't care less.' It was a narrative I was hearing everywhere and, like all narratives, the more we hear it, the more we believe it, even if we haven't gone to the trouble of fact-checking it. Everybody seemed to think, without ever having met the builder, that I would never see him again.

We tell ourselves stories to justify our emotions and our judgement

The more I heard these stories, the more I started to believe them, and the more I believed them, the more my anger and frustration grew. Each time I called the builder and didn't receive a call back I was getting more and more angry, and as my anger increased, so too did the narrative about the builder – that he was a cowboy, a crook, a criminal, disrespecting me. My frustration and anger were no longer caused by the few small issues to do with the building work; they were now the result of the inner story in my head about the builder and my interpretation of him not returning my calls. But when emotions take over, logic fails, and sometimes we don't care if our inner story is even true; if it perpetuates the emotion and justifies our actions, that's all we need.

When I finally got to speak with the builder on the phone my anger was at peak level, and as soon as he answered I decided to follow the advice in my head and give him a piece of my mind. Before he had time to speak, I unloaded my anger on him and told him that he had treated me totally unfairly, that he was a criminal and a crook and a cowboy and every other thing I could think of.

I spent the first few minutes unloading, unleashing all my anger and frustration on him and reminding him about the work he had done on my house and how important it was to get it right. At that moment I had made my anger and my pain the most important thing.

I will never forget the silence when I'd finished speaking. I was waiting for some kind of fight, I was committed to a fight, so I asked him, 'Are you there?'

Quietly and gently, he said, 'Yes, I am.'

And for the first time on the call I started to listen, and the moment I did so I knew I was wrong. I heard something in his voice that immediately cut through the nonsense in my head.

'I am here,' he said. 'I am sorry, Gerry, there is nothing I can do about it now. My wife has been very ill the last few months. She is passing away and I have spent the last two weeks sitting by her bedside.'

There was another silence then, filled with heartbreak and deep human pain.

'She is 36 years old,' he continued, 'we have two young kids and I have no idea how I'm going to cope without her. I am sorry for the problems, absolutely I will fix them but, right now, Gerry, I simply can't be there. I need to be here with my wife and my children.'

At that moment I learned one of the greatest lessons of my life. I learned how fast I could be to judge people and situations without any evidence and without taking the time to get to the bottom of the issue or to fact-check the story that I had allowed to build in my mind. I had allowed myself to spend two weeks in a state of anger and judgement while he had spent those weeks in heartbreak and pain.

If I'd been less willing to allow myself to be consumed by anger and judgement, I would have taken a different approach. I would have realised that the work, although it was important, wasn't life-threatening or life-changing; it didn't in any way impede or impact my ability to live my everyday life. The building work wasn't an issue for anybody else except me and for the story inside my head and the emotion inside my mind.

There was a story in my head, a deep-rooted story from my childhood, that I wasn't being taken seriously, that people were out to get me and that people saw me as a soft touch. My anger and frustration had nothing to do with the building work or even the builder. The builder had simply triggered a reservoir of anger and dysfunctional stories that I had been keeping in my mind since childhood. And now, when faced with the truth, I realised how much of a fool I had been and how disrespectful my judgement had been.

Had I maintained a sense of perspective and a sense of focus, I would have asked the builder, when eventually I spoke with him, if everything was OK because I had been unable to reach him. If I had changed my inner story, I would have changed my emotions. By releasing judgement, I would have waited to get the facts. And by starting the conversation with a different question, I might have been able to help someone in a very vulnerable state. But instead I allowed a dysfunctional story to build. I allowed a dysfunctional, destructive emotion to take over.

Press Pause

Take a moment to think of someone about whom you may have formed an opinion. What is the opinion and what evidence do you have to support that opinion? Is the evidence real, is it verified, have you checked it? Who has helped you to form this opinion – do they have expertise or special insight into the situation? When you think of the person about whom you hold the opinion – are you assessing the situation on its own merits or have you allowed a past experience to emotionally sabotage it; are you allowing an emotion from the past to flood into this one?

One of the greatest lessons I've learned is that at times we need to be patient. We need to fact-check the stories that are building in our head. We need to check the emotions we are holding and building and perpetuating and ask if they are helpful or hurtful. And we need to listen to the judgements in our head and ask if we are judging people or situations unfairly. Are we judging them too quickly? And are we judging them without a shred of evidence? Judgement of people and situations is one of the quickest routes to unhappiness, to anger and frustration.

Non-judgement is where we have the kindness, the patience to look for real answers, to wait for full clarity, to allow people and situations to unfold fully before we make a judgement call, before we allow a story to build and before we allow our emotions to blind us to the truth and trap us in a place of self-created pain.

The three major judgements are:

- Judgement of situation
- Judgement of others
- Judgement of self

Non-judgement means not getting caught up in our own ideas and opinions, likes and dislikes, in our own ego, to the point where we condemn all that is different to our own likes, expectations and opinions or where we label as wrong all that exists outside our own definitions of truth. Non-judgement enables us to be curious and to be open to new ideas, new ways of thinking and new ways of being. It enables us to look for the good and the elements of truth in all ideas and opinions and to keep a healthy openness and willingness to let go of certain elements of our own truths and thinking in order to form new ones. As mentioned above, there are three elements that we can be far too quick to judge – the situation, ourselves and others. In the section on beliefs, we learned that many of the beliefs and values we hold are ones we have downloaded from our parents, caregivers and society in order to be able to fit in. We were programmed to see everything that is different as a threat, which is simply not the case.

Most of us can go through our days consciously or unconsciously judging our experiences and situations, other people and ourselves, and most of us don't even realise we are doing this.

We live in a world where we are actively encouraged to 'like' or 'unlike' things we see online, to rate and respond to comments made and pictures posted by others. A world where we feel it is important to publicly give a thumbs up or down to places we've visited or experiences we've had, and often we think our rating is a true and objective fact, forgetting that we are simply expressing our own inner subjective interpretation.

We live in a world where we are encouraged to rate, to categorise and to judge almost everything we see. Immediately after an experience we label it as bad or great, but we seldom wait to see what learnings, insights or opportunities the experience will create in our lives before we do so. How many times have we had an experience we judged as bad only to realise months or years later that what happened was actually a blessing in disguise. When we break up with a partner we might judge this situation to be the biggest loss of our life yet six months later we meet the true love of our life. Or we might not get that job we coveted and judge ourselves to be lacking and 'less than'. Yet in time we discover that our true passion lies elsewhere or a better job more suited to us comes up.

The ancient wisdom traditions teach that the key to a happy existence is *not* to avoid 'mistakes' or unwanted situations but simply to let go of all judgement of them and surrender and commit to learning from the experience.

Judgement is our ego's primary reaction to a situation that causes it to feel challenged and/or threatened by the unplanned, the unfamiliar or the unexpected. The ego thrives on familiarity and will quickly judge everything else to be 'wrong' and not simply 'different'. Judgement in its truest form has of course a very important role; it is the natural means by which we determine threat and danger; it is a vital tool for survival. But this threat should be a threat to our lives; the danger is when we begin to see as threats the things that challenge our beliefs, our sense of self or our sense of self-derived status. Instead of using judgement to keep us physically alive we are now using it to keep us as the centre of attention, keep us popular, to maintain a sense of control and a sense of importance, and we are labelling or judging everything and anything or indeed anyone that challenges this as wrong.

We live in a world where people are forced to take sides in debates where it seems the common middle ground no longer exists, and we end up with two opposite sides, each fighting to be right, each trying to shout down the other, each saying the other is wrong, each unwilling to listen to the other – and when this happens the only thing that matters is which side wins, even if that means the truth, which often exists somewhere between the two polar opinions, is lost. In such a

'The truth is that no matter how hard we try to suppress these emotions, no matter how hard we try to avoid triggering situations, somebody or something is going to trigger them and when they do they can create chaos and personal pain.'

'When we let go of the burden of judgement, we find silence in our hearts.'

scenario the conversation disintegrates into an emotional, often self-serving battle to be right and not a humanity-serving debate to find truth. Judgement is the ego's method of defence; it creates immediate isolation and needs others to be wrong in order for us to be right.

Human experience shows us that the very things we judge as 'wrong' or 'bad' often bother us and consume our attention far more than the things we see as correct or good. And our attachment to and fixation on the things or people we see as wrong can have a negative impact on our lives, filling us with anger and comparison. Very often it is our constant – and often harsh and unkind – judgement of ourselves and others that is the root cause of our suffering. Our inner need to judge often stems from our inability or unwillingness to recognise, identify and address our own fear. We can even get to a point of judgement where we begin to blame others for our own anger and bitterness.

When we learn not to judge we open ourselves to new ideas and to expanding our belief systems. When we let go of the burden of judgement we find silence in our hearts.

Judgement doesn't have to be of other people or external situations, it can be of ourselves

Judgement can be directed outwards, at other people and external situations, but it can also be directed inwards. When something doesn't happen the way we wanted it to, we can perceive this as a failure. We can judge ourselves harshly and experience feelings of shame, anger, defensiveness, aggression and guilt. We can get to a point where we are judging ourselves, judging the person we are at this moment and the life we have at this moment against a fictional, self-created vision of the person we think we 'should' be or against the life we think we 'should' have. This can often be the saddest and worst form of judgement, which strips away all our self-worth, our self-confidence and our ability to see and experience the incredible abundance in our lives, the amazing stories in our life journey and the incredible characteristics in our personality.

The practice of non-judgement has the power to transform the way we see and experience the world. The important questions we need to ask once we become aware that we are judging are what would it be like to be free of judgement, to be free to allow others to be who they need to be and free to allow me to be who I need to be? What would it feel like to focus on the growth opportunity that the situation presents and no longer spend time and energy resisting the situation? What would it be like to have the ability to simply experience life, other people and myself without judgement?

For me, at the start of 2020, whether it was what I wanted or expected was irrelevant; what was important was what I did now, and the first thing I had to do in order to free up my time, my energy and my freedom was to let go of all the things that were not serving me – and judgement of the situation was the first that had to go. It was what it was; what it became was now up to me.

Press Pause

- *Where in your life are you judging something or somebody without actually having the facts?*
- *Where are you judging something too quickly without waiting to see how it might actually turn out?*
- *Where have you allowed your belief about the possible outcome impact your motivation?*
- *What would it take for you to release this judgement?*
- *What is the cost to you of this, most likely incorrect judgement?*
- *What can you focus on that would give you back a sense of empowerment?*
- *What would non-judgement look like?*
- *How would non-judgement allow you to feel?*
- *Are your inner stories right now ones of self-empowerment or disempowerment?*
- *What would a better story sound like?*
- *What would an empowered and emotionally aware person do in this situation?*
- *Who are you waiting for to give you the empowerment to release judgement?*

3. Non-attachment

Non-attachment does not mean that we have to be exempt or absent from emotions; it does not mean we have to exist as an emotionless entity – that would be to deny our humanity and the depth and range of human feelings and experiences. Feelings and emotions still exist in a state of non-attachment, feelings and emotions will still appear, but the difference is how we respond and relate to them and this will be based on our ability to observe the emotion, identify its true root cause and then decide whether we want to continue to experience that emotion or change it and whether we want to act from that emotion or not.

Even the most enlightened spiritual teachers are capable of laughing, crying, regretting, wishing, but they are also able to decide what they do with each emotion and how long they wish to hold each emotion. Non-attachment does not mean we never experience negative emotions or situations: it means we avoid getting entangled in them, losing perspective to them and losing our true self to them. As stated earlier, my belief is that emotions themselves are neither good nor bad, it's what we do with them, it's who we become with them, that defines whether they are good or bad. We can all experience anger but we don't have to act out of anger; we can all feel fear but we don't have to act out of fear. As described before, the ability to experience an emotion but not be distracted by it or consumed by it is the key. Non-attachment, or detachment, allows us to experience all emotions and with conscious awareness select the ones that are helpful and remove the others.

The things we emotionally attach our energy and attention to are either magnifying the problem or magnifying the solution and either enabling or disabling us.

Because, as we have seen, our brain is a threat-detection system, it is always looking to identify and magnify all the possible threats in our world. These can be real, imaginary or even remembered. In order to make sure we avoid them, the brain will try to generate a powerful emotion so that we keep focused on the potential threat and don't get distracted. In this situation we are psychologically and emotionally fixated on and dominated by the threats in the world, often to the exclusion of the opportunities. We literally develop psychological and emotional tunnel vision where we focus solely on the threat. The more we attach our energy and our attention to it, the bigger it gets and the more everything else fades out of our vision; we lose perspective, and we lose sight of the bigger picture.

Non-attachment to our inner stories

Non-attachment also means that we don't have to attach to our thoughts and inner stories. If we choose not to attach to our thoughts, we can observe them as the observer self, without judgement or resistance, and allow ourselves to either be curious about them or to simply let them go. As soon as we don't give our energy and attention to a thought, the signal being sent into the brain neuron dissipates and the thought subsides. As soon as a thought is no longer receiving an electrical charge, the emotion falls away. In order for our thoughts to persist they need us to keep poking them, agreeing with them, disagreeing with them – it doesn't matter, as long as we are giving them energy and attention. As soon as we detach from them they have no more power or control over us and subside quickly.

'Non-attachment means that we don't have to attach to our thoughts and inner stories.'

Press Pause

The next time you find yourself spiralling into anxious thoughts or catastrophising about something that may happen in the future, allow yourself to recognise the thought. Then imagine that thought is a balloon in your hand. Realise that you are holding onto the string of that balloon so tightly and firmly that your fist is almost sore from holding onto it. Now imagine yourself releasing that string. Watch the balloon, with that negative thought about some imagined event in the future, float away, releasing you from all attachment to it. Now notice how the body softens and relaxes; this is the somatic experience. When we practise non-attachment we not only free our minds from the pressure and strain, we also liberate our bodies to a place of ease and our souls to a place of peace.

Non-attachment has nothing to do with a fear of wealth or abundance

Non-attachment does not mean that we don't own anything: it means that nothing owns us. Non-attachment allows us to live in a manner that means we can have and receive nice things but our happiness, our identity and our self-worth are not attached to these things. The importance of something is simply defined by how much we attach our happiness, our identity or our meaning to it. When we detach our happiness, our identity and our meaning from these things it means our happiness is now built on and stemming from an inner reservoir that we can keep filled up without the need for these external things. Non-attachment does not stop us from enjoying the gift of nice things but gives us the freedom to enjoy them but not need them.

We are not our mistakes

With attachment, there is also the danger that we can attach our identity or our well-being to something that is happening outside of ourselves. Very often we can attach our identity and our sense of self, our sense of worth, to the things that we are doing or to the projects that we are involved in.

Think of a great footballer who on a particular day is not having a good game and in fact has just kicked the ball wide when it was easier to score. If the player is attached to the mistake, if his identity is attached to his performance, he will begin to ask, *What is wrong with me? Have I lost my skill? Maybe I'm not good enough. Will I get taken off? Do I even love this game anymore?*

A non-attached player, a player who has separated himself and his identity from his performance, asks totally different questions. He asks, *How do I get myself back into the game? What was the mistake I made that allowed me to kick the ball wide?* He looks at the mistake simply as a process that is external to himself and that he has the power to change. The non-attached player knows that class is permanent but form is temporary.

So even though he's having a bad game at that moment, he knows that the mistake he made is not a part of his permanent identity. His permanent identity is a strong, confident, professional player. It is important in our lives that we see the work that we do, the projects that we are involved in, as simply tasks and not an expression of our identity. It is important that we don't attach our identity or a sense of self to those tasks.

When we are involved in a project that isn't working out, when there are things in our life that we have failed in, it is so important that we view them as external projects, that we review the process behind the task and see the perceived failure as simply a process that didn't work. And by not attaching our permanent identity to this temporary reality, we maintain the inner sense that we are competent, confident and capable people.

It is vital that we don't attach our identity, our beautiful eternal permanent identity, to temporary tasks.

Talent, genius, kindness and love are permanent, form is temporary, and every single one of us at some point in our life will make mistakes, we will struggle with tasks, we will get tasks wrong, but it is important in those moments that we remember who we are. It is important that we remember the greatest successes that we've had, the challenges we've overcome, the tests that we've completed. It is so important that we don't begin to attach a permanent eternal identity to a temporary reality.

I am currently working with an incredible athlete, a sailor. He competes in the world's biggest off-shore races, and at sea, as you can imagine, there are so many factors he can't control and as these factors change he has to make split-second decisions to respond as quickly as he can. Often the decision he makes is wrong and he immediately knows that this might cost him serious time or position.

As soon as we become aware that we have made a bad decision, it is easy get caught up in anger and frustration. Instead, we can work on a very simple strategy called 'accept and act'. The 'accept' is to accept our decision without emotion, recognise it was the wrong one and then immediately put our awareness, attention and emotion into the action to resolve the mistake. The mistake is not the issue: the issue is often our response to the mistake. If we are attached to the mistake, then we stay in the mistake, we stay in the problem, but if we are not attached to the mistake, we are no longer in the problem, we are in the solution, and in switching our attachment we are no longer magnifying the problem, we are magnifying the solution.

BENEFITS OF NON-ATTACHMENT

Once you are able to embrace, accept and detach from your emotions, you will experience some incredible benefits such as:

- Your life will no longer be ruled by changing emotions or expectations.
- You will experience more inner space even with all your existing emotions.
- You can observe and relate to the world in a whole

---

new way. You will start seeing and experiencing it as it actually is, instead of based solely on your own inner concepts and emotions.

- You will worry less about things, situations and people you can't control. Things and scenarios around you will have less impact on you.

- You will become more compassionate as you move away from the emotion of anger.

- You will be genuinely happy – if you practise detachment, you will be satisfied with what you have. You get the chance to enjoy what is present, instead of running after happiness desperately.

- You will let your life unfold and flow naturally and realise there is no need for you to control all the things around you.

- You will continue to choose and experience love. Loving will become a natural part of you and the thing that you consciously choose, by consciously choosing not to be defined by anger, bitterness, judgement or hatred.

- You will feel free. This feeling of freeing up internal space and freedom is the greatest gift to the self. This makes it easier for you to be content with everything that's happening to you right now. Non-attachment makes you embrace freedom because it gives you the chance to have full control over your emotions and your mind, instead of the other way around. This form of freedom makes it possible for you to enjoy all your experiences without any form of disappointment or frustration.

Press Pause

Can you think of a situation you are attached to that is causing you pain and unhappiness? This might be a person, something that someone did to you or a hurt that you've experienced.

Is your attachment empowering or disempowering you? Is it healing you or hurting you?

What if you were to take your attention and focus from that situation or person and place it back on you and your response to that person?

Are you attaching your energy and attention to your place of pain or your place of power?

Where is your power in this situation?

What would an emotionally free person do in this situation?

What would it take to allow yourself to detach your energy and attention from that person or situation?

By taking your energy and attention away from what's hurting you, you will have greater energy and attention to give to something that will heal and empower you – what is this?

Can you give yourself permission to be emotionally free from this person or situation?

4. Non-striving

Think of striving as a strong inner desire to reach a particular outcome such as a relationship, a job, a salary, an accomplishment. The word desire is important here and if you investigate what a desire is, for example the desire to eat, there is often a strong physiological or neurological mechanism underlining it and supporting it. We must be aware that our desires can also change us at a chemical and neurobiological level, which is a really important aspect when we begin to observe and understand not just the desire but the impacts and consequences that desire has on our health and happiness. A powerful desire is not a bad or a good thing: it's the changes it makes to the person holding the desire that makes it good or bad; it's who we become while holding the desire that matters. The concept of 'non-striving' welcomes, acknowledges and even honours the desire and also allows us to observe and investigate it on a deeper level.

We can ask ourselves if the desire we are holding is bringing us joy, love and peace or bringing impatience and frustration and taking us out of the moment and away from the happiness and abundance that is present right now. We can ask ourselves if the desire we are holding is creating extra tension, pressure and suffering.

Non-striving is the ability to consciously hold a future intent, a future image and a future goal without taking us out of the beauty and possibility that

> **'Non-striving is the ability to consciously hold a future intent, a future image and a future goal without taking us out of the beauty and possibility that exists in each and every step towards the outcome.'**

exists in each and every step towards the outcome. Think of a sportsperson, a highly motivated and ambitious football player who wants to win the World Cup. They can hold this clear intent, this clear desired future goal that inspires them and motivates them, and at the same time they can be fully focused, committed and present not just in each game on the journey towards that goal but also to each play and each moment in each game. The player works to improve their skills and concentrates on being the right player with the right process in the moment. In fact, if they are too focused on the outcome and try to rush the process they are far less likely to achieve their goal.

Striving is an over-attachment to outcome, an uneasiness in the present moment. Non-striving involves trying less and being more. It is about focusing less on chasing our goals and more on creating and maintaining the mindset and the emotional conditions that will enable us to achieve them. In writing this book I had to become fully invested in it, giving it time, effort and hard work, but once this book goes out into the world I knew that I had to release it, I had to practise non-attachment to outcome. That's not to say that I don't care about it but I know that I did my best and put the effort into the areas that I could control. Non-attachment to outcome means letting go, knowing that we have done the best we could.

Non-striving does not mean we don't pursue dreams and goals, of course we do; everything in the universe is changing all the time so not changing and not evolving is not a healthy thing. The practice of non-striving is to *put some space* between ourselves and the desire to reach our goals so that this desire doesn't control us, and we remain free to both consciously pursue the future and enjoy the process and the journey that will lead us there.

Non-striving is the ability to be at peace and ease with things as they are along the way to manifesting our dreams and goals. By not striving we are allowing ourselves to be more open along the path, more open to new ideas, new opportunities, alternate paths, and less worried or attached to a certain outcome. Too often in life we arrive at an outcome only to realise the journey to the outcome was full of fear, anxiety, racing and pushing and that we didn't really enjoy it or, even worse, that the journey cost us our happiness, distracted us from what was important, took us away from our values, cost us our relationships or even our health. Far too often I've heard of people who have qualified and even medalled at the Olympic Games yet after returning home have said they didn't really enjoy the games, that it was all a process of stress, pressure and sacrifice that did not lead to greater happiness. On the other hand, those Olympic athletes who returned home from the games and said it was the most enjoyable experience in their life have actually gained something far more precious than a medal. They have gained a life experience of fun, joy and passion. The same could be said for business goals. Far too many people spend years chasing goals and promotions in a state of fear and stress, and this has such a cost in terms of happiness and their personal life that even when they achieve their goal there is an air of regret or sorrow. Life is short, time is precious. Putting

'Taking our emotional power back from the outcome and placing it in the process allows us to bring our entire energy and attention into the current moment and allows us to commit with greater clarity, focus, enthusiasm and passion.'

up with constant unhappiness in pursuit of some distant perceived happiness is never a good exchange.

Very often if we are in an emotional state of fear or anxiety we can look at a possible outcome through the lens of this emotion and we can create a fictional outcome that disempowers us, demotivates us or causes us emotional stress. The more we become consumed by emotions relating to the outcome, the more we lose sight of the process, and when we lose sight of the process the chances of the outcome we fear are increased and we end up fulfilling our own beliefs, not because our prediction was correct but because our emotional attachment to the outcome created an emotion that didn't allow us to really commit to the process and to really shine in the way we could have. Taking our emotional power back from the outcome and placing it in the process allows us to bring our entire energy and attention into the current moment and to commit with greater clarity, focus, enthusiasm and passion. And when we start to generate these emotions, the process itself become the exciting part and the part to which we are attached, and the more we focus on the right process and the more we fill the process with clarity, focus, enthusiasm and passion, the more likely the outcome is going to be the one we want. It sounds almost counter-intuitive but to achieve our desired outcome we are far better attaching our energy and attention to the process. In my experience, if an outcome was achieved through fear, stress and worry, it was not worth it. We have all heard the expression that it's all about the process and not the outcome, and yet so many people are attached to the outcome and either missing the process or not enjoying it. My belief is that a goal or an outcome is only valuable if the process to get it has made us grow and come alive in a healthy way. Otherwise it has simply robbed us of our valuable time.

The right person with the right process never worries about the outcome

Through my work, I have gained an absolute belief that the right person, with the right process, never has to worry about the outcome. Yet many people spend so much of their life worrying about the outcome, afraid to take the first step until they have some kind of proof that the outcome will happen, or frantically chasing an outcome in a way that is making them unhappy and unhealthy, or chasing the right outcome with the wrong process.

While working at a football club, I was lucky enough to get to know and to work with one of the greatest players in the world, and possibly one of the greatest of all time. There is no doubt that in my time there I learned far more from him than he did from me. But in working with him we developed a model that I have used with multiple athletes at world, European and Olympic level and many successful corporate teams. It's a very simple and powerful model that we can apply to so many situations in life.

The player in question has to make high-impact decisions in split seconds about when and where he kicks. These kicks can be from any angle, in any weather. The angle of the kick, the position of the other players, the distance from goal, the time left on the clock, and the scoreboard all combine to ensure that no two kicks are ever the same yet there is a level of consistency that is demanded from the player. But what really makes things so difficult is the psychological and emotional pressure that that player is under. Vital kicks, such as penalties, may come at the end of a game when the player has already expended all his mental, physical and emotional energy. They may come in terrible pitch conditions or very difficult weather conditions. Thousands of people watching in the stadium and millions watching all around the world are focused on the player's every move and half of those people are willing him to miss the penalty. All of his teammates are desperately watching and hoping and often he alone bears the responsibility of the winning or losing of the game.

The expectations and the pressure are on that player to put the ball exactly where it is meant to end up, between the goalposts. But while everybody was watching, hoping, anticipating and attached to the outcome, which is the score, this player had an incredible ability to take his mental and emotional focus away from the outcome and instead place it on the process, the pre-shot routine and the kick routine. Over the years he had developed a very detailed pre-kick routine that allowed all his focus and energy to be channelled into this process and very little if any into the outcome. He focused so much on the physical, mental and emotional process that he used to say once he took the penalty, once the ball left his foot, 'It's nothing to do with me anymore.' To show how much he believed and practised this, the moment he executed a penalty kick, he would turn and run back up the pitch with his back to the ball. He would not stand waiting and hoping for the outcome. If he was to stand every time, waiting for the ball to hit the back of the net, he would be placing more emotional charge on the outcome than the process. He had to ensure that at every moment, in every game, his emotional attachment was always on the process; he learned how to become detached from the outcome.

What we noticed was even though the process was perfectly executed, perfectly defined and perfectly rehearsed, sometimes it didn't work. We noticed that at times the process on one kick could work and later the process on another kick wouldn't work.

There was another variable, another factor that was impacting the process and the outcome. This other factor we came to define as 'The person'.

The process is driven by the person; the pre-kick routine or the pre-kick process is only as good as the quality of the mind that is executing it. So while he had focused on developing an incredible process, now we also had to develop an incredible mindset and a way of using internal triggers to get himself quickly into this psychological and emotional space of clarity, calmness, focus and self-belief. No matter what his psychological or emotional state was before the penalty was awarded – and often he would be frustrated, tired or distracted – he had little time to change this and use what we call internal regulation to alter his psychological and emotional state. With the player, we began to look at things like calmness, composure, focus, noise, distraction, spatial awareness, depth, perception, ability to withstand distraction. We identified all the key physical, mental and emotional characteristics that he needed to have and then each and every day we went about training those skills. We were giving no emotional or mental energy or attachment to outcome. But every day we focused on two things – right person, right process; right person, right process – so long in advance of that vital game-winning kick, he knew the mental and emotional skills that he would need to execute the process excellently. And because we had worked, measured and demonstrated the strength of those skills, again and again in training, he could step up to that stage with massive belief in himself and massive belief in the process.

In any sport, in any business, it is so important to have a clear process and clear systems that drive performance and drive the outcome. It is equally important to have incredible people who can execute the process excellently. In any walk of sport, business or life, those same two things are really important: right person, right process. The right person with the right process rarely concerns themselves with the outcome. Yet in sport, in business and in life, we often get so consumed with the outcome, we strive to the outcome, we push, we force to the outcome and we can often abandon and forget the process and the person. How many companies are chasing numbers, chasing KPIs, chasing results but not always with the greatest process and with team members who are tired, distracted, overworked, too busy? Too many companies say that people are the most important thing yet the things they measure and obsess about are outcomes.

How many people in life are desperately seeking something, striving towards something and it's just not happening? The more we give the outcome our mental or emotional energy, the less mental or emotional energy we have for the other two factors, which are actually more important: right person, right process. Whatever we want in life, whatever life we want to manifest, we need to identify first and foremost the type of person that could achieve those things, the type of person that would have that success and the type of person that would be able to live the life we dream of. We must also define what a person who already has everything we desire would feel like, the emotions that would drive them. The more we start to experience the excitement and gratitude as if they have already happened, the more we are energetically attracting these things to us and the more we are sending an important message to the universe that we are ready to receive them. Any outcome, if

> 'Instead of focusing on outcome, put your time, energy and focus into making sure that you are turning up in the right way, with the right mindset, in the right emotional space and executing the right process.'

pursued with joy, excitement and fun, is far more likely to manifest. Long before we achieve the outcome, we must have the correct process, and long before we have the right process, we must become the right person.

Very often if we focus too much on the outcome we can become impatient, agitated and frustrated as we pursue our desired end, and the very fact that we have become impatient, agitated and frustrated is inhibiting us from thinking clearly, from being creative and insightful, and this state of being is blocking our inner knowing and insight and therefore actually preventing us from achieving the excellence or outcome we desire.

Instead of focusing on outcome, put your time, energy and focus into making sure that you are turning up in the right way, with the right mindset, in the right emotional space and executing the right process. Very often when we stop striving, when we stop rushing and racing, we discover opportunities and destinations along the way that are far more exciting and more powerful than the ones we initially set out to find.

Sometimes the biggest win comes in the learning and the growth

When we can eliminate the destructive emotions, see winning and losing as a pursuit of growth and learning and become attached to the growth and learning and not to the outcome, not to the victory or defeat, then we are emotionally free to play from a place of love and joy. In order to do this, we need to eradicate the voice of the inner critic. We cannot be defined by the sport or the goal we are chasing; our identity is far bigger than the thing we are pursuing and if our happiness and peace are dependent on that outcome then the outcome owns us. The goals we pursue, the outcomes we desire, are not our identity. Our identity is so much more, so much bigger, so much more important.

Understanding what we fear is to understand all that imprisons us in the pursuit of excellence and the life we dream of. We all, at times, think we fear failure, but in my experience we can all overcome failure easily when we are not attached to or defined by that failure or perception of failure. But what we struggle to overcome sometimes is the inner voice that comes alive, the stories we tell ourselves and the emotions we experience after the failure. I have come to realise that in life, you win or you learn, and as long as you are learning, as long as you are growing, as long as you are staying emotionally liberated from the outcome, then there is no fear.

It is important that we can emotionally put our challenges in a perspective box, that we don't deny them, don't run away from them, and that we make sure we give them only the space in our life that they deserve and know that our challenges or the outcomes we are pursuing do not define us and will never define us. Our victories and our defeats do not define who we are. It's how we think and act and respond in the face of both victory and defeat that matters and this response is either imprisoning us or liberating us. It is

> '**As long as you are growing, as long as you are staying emotionally liberated from the outcome, then there is no fear.**'

our ability to win and lose and all the while remain free from the win or loss that is the greatest of all abilities in life and in sport.

Long before we can achieve an outcome, we must become the type of person who has already achieved that outcome, and we have to have a process that will work towards that outcome. What I've learned absolutely in my life is that the universe is 50 per cent and we are 50 per cent of the outcome. We are co-creators, we are not total creators. We have to work with the universe and at times the universe will challenge and test us, at times things won't appear to be working. It is at those moments that we must stay emotionally calm and focused and in those moments we go back to change either the process or the type of person we are turning up as every day – or we change both. But we never change our dream.

The other part of non-striving is to notice just how much of our time is spent striving: striving to wake up early, to be productive, to earn money, to find love, to exercise, to eat healthily. We can spend vast amounts of our life in this mode of constant striving, constant goal-setting and constant doing and not enough time in the moment. It is only in the present moment that all opportunities to be happy, to love and to be at peace exist.

Non-striving also means *experiencing far more presence* in our lives, where we are fully present with ourselves and the people we love. We are there, in the moment, without needing to change it. We are present without any agenda. Non-striving allows us to enter, expand and be at ease in the space between the no longer and the not yet.

EMBRACING THE SPACE BETWEEN
THE NO LONGER AND THE NOT YET

At a certain moment each day, the morning meets the night and for that moment it's neither morning nor night: it's just the universe being itself without our human labels and without the human need to be in one defined place or another. Like the cycle of day and night, in all our journeys there are periods of in-between, moments where the old is about to fade away forever and the new has not yet appeared. In these moments we need patience, ease and trust. In these moments we have to be willing to lose sight of the shores of the familiar when we cannot yet see the shores of our new destination. Just like a sailor sailing beyond the horizon to new lands, who has to trust in his vessel, his map and his navigation, we must at times let go of the old long before the new comes into view. Like the sailor, we too must have great trust in ourselves and in our ability to navigate our way through adversity or distraction.

We can only enjoy these moments between the no longer and the not yet when we are ready and willing to surrender to them and let go of striving. A sailor must be patient and work with the timelines provided to him by the ocean, the wind and the tides. We too must surrender to the greater and higher power of the universe and sometimes allow things to unfold in their own time. Just like the sailor focuses on maintaining a good vessel, a good crew, a good navigation system, we must be willing to follow our own process, and commit to our daily habits and good practice, but we must also be patient and know that we can't always control when things happen or exactly how long it will take to get us from the harbour of the old to the shores of the new. In these moments, between the no longer and the not yet, the universe is asking us to simply:

- Be patient
- Be awake
- Be at ease
- Commit to good practices

Press Pause

When you look at all your deepest life desires, ask yourself what would the person who already had these in their life look like, think like, behave like?

When you describe that person, is that you?

What would the person who had already achieved your dreams say they attached their energy to?

How important would they say the process is?

How good is your process?

If you had all these things in your life, what emotions would you feel? Are you feeling these emotions now?

RIGHT PERSON	RIGHT PROCESS	RIGHT OUTCOME
Describe in five words the type of person that would achieve your goals.	List five process steps that lead to each listed outcome.	List the things you want to achieve.

5. Forgiveness

Forgiveness can be defined as a conscious and voluntary internal process of letting go of thoughts and emotions such as anger, resentment and bitterness. At various times we will be called to forgive ourselves, others and the universe. Forgiveness will ask us to give up the need and the right for revenge towards someone who we believe has hurt us. This can of course be ourselves who has hurt us or let us down. The more we learn to forgive ourselves, the easier life becomes and the more the past dissolves, leaving us with a renewed ability to be present. Forgiveness helps us to not hold onto grudges and mistakes. True forgiveness involves accepting that our mistakes matter but that so too does our suffering, our health and our happiness. Forgiveness, of self, of others or of the universe, is first and foremost for our own growth and happiness.

At times in life we have every right to be angry, to be bitter, we have every right to be frustrated, but we also have a powerful freedom to move beyond these hurtful emotions. When we hold onto hurt, pain, resentment and anger it harms us far more than we may know and can even harm us more than it harms the offender. Holding anger towards someone else is like putting our hand into a fire and holding a hot coal so that when we see the person we are angry with we have something to burn them with; but all the while we are the ones being burnt the most. Forgiveness frees us to live in the present with a new emotion of ease and peace and growth. We have to learn to forgive ourselves, again, and again.

Forgiveness does not erase the past; it absolutely acknowledges it and accepts it for what it is but looks upon it with compassion. Forgiveness is not about forgetting what took place, or condoning or excusing the offence; it is simply making a powerful, conscious choice to reframe it and to be emotionally free from it to the point where that person, that situation, no longer occupies any space in our emotional world. We can become emotionally free from the past by releasing all emotional and energetic connections to it that are keeping us locked in an inner negative emotion. Forgiveness allows us to release our attachment to that which is holding us in a place of pain.

Forgiveness of others starts with acknowledging that someone has done something wrong to us, acknowledging the pain or hurt it has caused, and can also involve acknowledging that we in no part deserved it. Forgiveness is not always easy, in fact it can be very hard; the easy thing is to stay angry, but by doing so we can never free ourselves to become our true and authentic self. We must be willing to release all that no longer serves us, accept what has been and has to be with ease and grace, and embrace what is to be and who you can be with love and compassion. Forgiveness liberates the soul and sets us free.

Press Pause

Is there a person or situation that you are holding anger and hurt towards?

What is the impact that holding this anger and hurt is having on you?

What is the real need that might begin to allow you to let go of this?

Do you want this person or situation to have this control over your emotional state and your happiness?

Is it time to take away all emotions and power from that person or situation?

Is there a part of yourself or your past you need to forgive?

What would no longer holding these emotions feel like?

What is the positive impact that releasing these emotions would have on you and your life?

How long will you wait to release them?

What would the first step in forgiveness look like?

---

6. Non-comparison

Non-comparison is where we begin to realise a very important fact – that no one has ever lived our life before, everyone is on their own journey and in that journey we all have different destinations. Without keeping these simple facts to the front of our mind, we can easily get caught up in comparing ourselves to others, comparing our journey to theirs and comparing our destination to theirs. Two people can be in completely different places in life and both can be in the right place. The right place is not an objective place, but a subjective place that has to be right for the person that is in it. An example: one person might chose to pursue a master's degree, while their friend chooses to take a year travelling the world. Either decision is neither right or wrong, good or bad. The decision is right if it meets the emotional needs of that person at that time.

We can also be guilty of comparing the outward look of other lives to the internal feelings in our own life. We all experience our own lives from the inside, the everyday ups and downs and the everyday emotions, but we experience other people's lives from outside and without the feelings that are involved. When actors are making movies, the shooting is done in millions of micro moments and often not in sequence. An actor friend of mine has starred in lots of movies. When he explains the process and the feeling of making a movie, the hard work, the endless waiting, I realise that being an actor and being the person that watches the movie are two very different things. In one of his movies there was an incredible heartwarming scene that was the picture of happiness. I asked him what it was like to shoot it, thinking he would say it was amazing, joyful, love-filled, the reason he got into acting.

'Terrible,' he said. 'We were there for days trying to get that shot, the weather was awful, we had to take it over and over again and everything was going against us. By the time we finally got the shot we were all exhausted, we just wanted to get out of there and we'd had enough of each other.' He said it was a moment where he asked himself if this was what he wanted to do. 'We didn't even think the scene would make the final cut so we really couldn't see the point. It frustrated everyone.'

I asked him if he felt differently when he finally saw the movie.

'Not really,' he said. 'I was delighted the movie worked but my memory of that scene was how miserable we all felt.'

I have another friend who has successfully climbed Mount Everest and he has an amazing photo taken by a fellow climber of one of the tents they slept in on their way. It's a famous part of the mountain, just before the summit and on a spectacular ledge. The picture shows the tent in the most amazing, snow-covered landscape, with a beautiful glow inside it from the light they used for warmth, and in the background is the sun rising on Mount Everest. It's one of the most striking photos I have ever seen.

When he first showed me the photo he asked, 'What do you think I feel when I see that picture?'

'We can only experience our own life through inner experience.'

Lost for enough powerful words I said, 'Pride, excitement, wonder?'

'When I see that picture,' he said, 'my stomach turns and all I can smell is piss.'

I was dumbfounded. 'What?'

'That area where the tent is, is close to where everyone goes to the toilet and there is the most disgusting smell of human urine there. But you have to camp there and all the time you are literally in the middle of a human toilet. And while I was in that tent I had the worst dose of altitude sickness ever, I had diarrhoea all night, I never felt so sick or so weak in all my life and all I wanted to do was get off the mountain. Every time I see that photo I feel sick and all I can smell is piss.'

Without the inner experience of the picture, we can look at other people's lives and see them for something they absolutely are not. We can only experience our own life through inner experience. That is why everyone else's life looks different to ours; we *feel* our lives but we see other people's lives.

Don't compare the real you to a fictional you

Non-comparison is also about not comparing ourselves to the person we think we should be or the person we used to be. Very often we compare ourselves to a fictional character that we create in our head or that someone has created in their head, and we spend our lives comparing the person we are to the fictional person someone directly or indirectly influenced us into thinking we should be. Life is a dynamic and constantly unfolding reality and so are we. Very often we have to accept life and the moment for what it is and surrender what we thought it would be. The ability to be at peace with the moment that is without resistance or judgement is one of the greatest freedoms there is. The ability to accept ourselves exactly as we are in this moment without judgement or resistance is another vital part of non-comparison and emotional freedom.

Press Pause

Is there someone you are comparing yourself to?

Why do you really compare yourself to this person?

Is this comparison bringing you happiness?

Are you comparing yourself to what you see on the outside without actually knowing their inner reality?

What would releasing this comparison do for you?

Are you comparing yourself to a fictional character you think you can be?

Who created this fictional character and why?

Are you comparing your life to a fictional life you think you 'should' have?

Who created this fictional life vision? Why is that vision important?

If you were in that fictional life, would you actually be happier? Would it really change how you feel on the inside?

When will you let the habit of comparison go?

---

7. Trust

Trust is about having confidence, faith or hope in someone or something. An example of trust is believing that the sun will rise in the morning. Trust means that even when life is happening in a way that is unexpected or unwanted, we have an inner knowing that there is a reason and a meaning for why it is happening the way it is, and this enables us to respond to what is happening with an open mind and a sense of curiosity instead of resistance and judgement. But it can be very difficult to trust in these moments, it can be hard to see the bigger picture, and that is because the only thing that we have when there is no trust is fear, and fear can imprison us into resistance and judgement.

In order to eliminate the fear that is imprisoning us we must first understand what we are really afraid of

There is a beautiful expression that says, 'Hot air balloons don't fly just because of the hot air in the balloon – they fly because the ropes that tie them to the ground have been cut'. Many of us have incredible ideas, dreams and life visions yet very often these ideas, dreams and visions never take flight. The vision, the passion, the belief, the enthusiasm that lift our dreams are so important – but these things alone will not enable our ideas, dreams and visions to fly if we have some kind of emotional fear or rope tying us to the ground.

In order to create a new life, a new way of living and a new way of feeling, we must liberate ourselves completely from the past and from every emotion that doesn't allow our dreams to fly. Very often when we think of our dreams and our ambitions, we tend to do two things: we overestimate the size of the challenge, and we underestimate our ability. The strongest emotion that ties us to the ground is fear and the first step towards eliminating fear is identifying what we are actually afraid of. It is my belief that what we fear most is that we are not enough. But the question we need to ask is 'Enough for who?' The moment we become enough for ourselves – the moment we look in the mirror and know that the person looking back is the only person who gets to have a say in the matter, and the moment we realise that daring to go after our dreams, having the courage to stand up and stand out and having the bravery to listen to our hearts, makes us enough there and then – we are free. It's time to trust ourselves to go after our dreams, and trust ourselves that no matter what happens we will meet ourselves with love and kindness.

Press Pause

Think of a string of pearls. Every pearl looks the same, and the beauty of the string has nothing to do with one particular pearl but with the string as a whole. We must think of life in the same way. We tend to give the life experiences that have the most emotions the most importance and make all the others less important. But the truth is that every single day and every single journey is connected and we need to learn to trust that we will all end where we are supposed to be.

Take my own life, for example. I would say the day I got married or the births of my two children were the biggest and most important moments of my life. But let's look further. In order to have those experiences I had to first meet my wife. In order to meet my wife, I had to first meet her brother, which would put in motion the destiny of me meeting my wife. But let's go a little deeper: how did I meet her brother? One day while visiting my parents I picked up a newspaper and the page I happened to open featured a story about a guy who had gone to Africa and set up a charity. He was a sportsperson so as a sports fan I was naturally interested. I read the article and found it fascinating, then put the paper down to have tea with my parents and thought no more of it. But somewhere in my mind his name was floating around.

A few weeks later I was rushing to get a flight to Beijing with a cycling team and my phone rang. I didn't recognise the number but thought it might be something to do with the trip so I answered. Would you believe, it was the guy I'd been reading about (my wife's brother) asking if I had time to meet for a chat. I had never spoken to him before that. I didn't have any space for new clients and only that I had read the article and was fascinated by him I would have said no. So I said yes, and we agreed to meet when I got back. But how did he get my number? Well, little did I know that his other sister had attended a talk I gave and had suggested he should call me. So maybe my wife's sister's decision to attend that talk was actually the point at which my life changed.

The funny thing is on the day of the talk I had decided I wasn't going to do it; my flight was in late and I wanted to go home and rest, and I picked up my phone a few times to cancel but something told me not to. I can still remember the exact moment when I came to the junction on the motorway where I would turn off for home but something changed inside me and at the last minute I decided to stay on the road. Every single day we make decisions and do things that can change the direction of our lives, sometimes destined to have a massive impact. And most of the time we don't give it any thought.

The string of pearls analogy reminds me that when we take our emotion out of it and see each day as a new opportunity and realise that everything we do is setting something in motion, we can begin to trust and to see the beauty and importance in our life moments and it reminds us not to get too caught up in particular moments because we can never really know how it will all play out.

---

8. Gratitude

In the pursuit of more, never forget the much we already have

One of the most powerful emotions we can experience is gratitude yet it is the one we tend to experience least. Many of us are told to constantly set targets and goals and chase new things, and while this can be exciting and motivating, it can mean that we are always looking towards the thing we want to manifest, which also means we are focusing on what we don't have and we lose sight of the many great things we have right here, right now.

The more we focus on things we don't have, the more we generate and start to live from an energy of lack or limitation that is constantly saying to the universe, 'I need more'. We can convince ourselves that what we have isn't enough or is somehow unwanted. Once we send this energy into the universe, telling it that what we have isn't wanted, the intelligent universe will do the logical thing – it will take what we have away.

There is a powerful expression that says, 'Tomorrow we will only be left with the things we expressed gratitude for today'. Gratitude enables us to become more aware of all the things we have right now, however big or small. A warm bed, a hot cup of tea, food in the fridge – these are things we can easily take for granted. When we begin to live from an emotion of gratitude, we begin to live from an energy of abundance and gratitude.

Living from an emotion of gratitude enables us to experience the kindness, the goodness and the gifts in our everyday lives in a whole new way. It allows us to let go of the need for constant striving and chasing and replaces it with an ability to extract the most amount of joy out of each and every moment as it unfolds. When we live from a place of gratitude we surrender the fear of not having enough and not being enough, and by surrendering fear we are releasing the fear chemicals and hormones out of our body and replacing them with hormones of gratitude and love.

Experiencing gratitude and taking time to express gratitude every single day is scientifically proven to lower cortisol levels and heighten levels of our feel-good hormone oxytocin.

'When we begin to live from an emotion of gratitude, we begin to live from an energy of abundance and gratitdue.'

This switch in our neurotransmitters has a powerful impact on our health and happiness. When practised regularly, gratitude can have an amazing effect on our chemistry, our biology and our brain activity, producing feelings of contentment and joy that are linked to physiological changes at the neurotransmitter level. When we express gratitude, our brains release the neuro-transmitters dopamine and serotonin. These are responsible for our emotions, and they make us feel safe and at ease. They enhance our mood, allowing us to feel happy from the inside.

By consciously practising gratitude we can help these neural pathways to strengthen themselves and ultimately create a permanent grateful and positive pathway within our brain activity and function. Gratitude has a powerful and positive impact on body functions and psychological conditions and can reduce conditions like stress, anxiety and depression.

By consciously practising gratitude, we can train the brain to attend selectively to positive emotions and thoughts, and thus we can actively reduce anxiety.

As humans, we can say many powerful things: *I love you*; *I forgive you*; *I am sorry*; *Thank you*. When we live our lives with gratitude, we appreciate what we have and move our focus from the things we don't have; we stop thinking about the things that are not yet in our lives and instead we say 'thank you'. Thank you to the universe for what it has given us, thank you for the people in our lives that love us, thank you to ourselves for always showing up for us, for sticking in there even during the difficult times and for daring to live and daring to love. Sometimes we can say thank you to our incredible bodies, our hearts, lungs, liver, kidneys, hands, feet, eyes. The truth is that gratitude is a powerful force, a powerful place from which we can begin to experience more joy and happiness in our lives, and it also enables us to experience better physical and mental health.

It is not happiness that brings us gratitude. It is gratitude that brings us happiness.

We live with an amazing system, an amazing combination of biology, chemistry and consciousness. Sometimes we are so busy, so distracted by the outside world, that we forget to acknowledge and say 'thank you' to our incredible body. The more we learn to say thank you, and the more we begin to see all the wonderful things other people do and all the wonderful things we do, and acknowledge it on a daily basis, the more we send that vibration frequency of gratitude into the universe. It could be when we purchase something in a shop, or meet someone as they get off a bus, or somebody just enters our space, our energy field, for a moment and we acknowledge them. We acknowledge the work they do; we acknowledge the way they have turned up. Maybe somebody asks a simple question, 'How are you?' It's easy just to say, 'Fine', but if we add a 'thank you' it's such a simple but powerful thing. We thank the universe, we thank the people around us, we thank our incredible systems within, our biology, our chemistry. We thank our amazing mind and each day as we encounter other human beings, in so many big and small ways during our day, we cultivate a habit of saying 'Thank you'. Two powerful and beautiful words, and the more we say them the more we radiate from a different mindset and the more we live from a different vibrational frequency.

Press Pause

Each day, take a few minutes to reflect on and write down three things you are grateful for. These can be big or small things, such as moments of joy, accomplishments or acts of kindness you've experienced. By regularly acknowledging and appreciating the positive aspects of your life, you can enhance your sense of gratitude and overall well-being

---

9. The emotional power of why

It was December 2022, our second child was three months old and we'd had 12 weeks of sleepless nights. For whatever reason, the universe had decided that this was not a time to sleep and our little girl was obliging the universe by keeping us awake all night.

In addition, I was trying to spend a lot of time with our little boy, who was three years old, making sure that he was adjusting to the new reality in our lives and the new energy and new soul that had entered the energy field that is our home.

And I was running a business that was quickly expanding and evolving, with a number of key personnel changes. It seemed to be all happening at once and, while it was all great, it was overwhelming. It had been an amazing year, an amazing few months of incredible life experience, but because of the output of energy that I had given, the arrival of a new little girl and 12 weeks of sleepless nights, I was feeling fatigued.

On my way into one of my sessions with my mentor Ravi, who as you know had already played such an important role in my life, I was on a phone call with one of the people in our business. We had just launched a major new event where we would hire a thousand-seater arena to put on an amazing show of talks, meditation, music and dance. Our plan was to fill the arena with energy and passion and create an environment of hope, connection and inspiration for people.

But for some reason the ticket sales were slow. I would later discover why, but a this point, however, it seemed there was little interaction with the event and before we got behind it and really gave it a marketing push we needed to decide if it would actually go ahead or if we would pull it. We'd had a really successful year, and the business had already hit all its targets, and from a personal point of view we now had two young children. So perhaps the decision should be to cancel the show, refund the tickets and run it at a better time.

In my brain, this made perfect sense, but deep down there was a hesitation, an inability to make that obvious decision, but I didn't know why. At Ravi's I was lying on the bed and he was working away in his usual quiet, reserved way.

But he sensed that there was something disturbing me. 'You are not at peace, Gerry,' he said.

'I'm not,' I replied.

'Tell me what is disturbing your peace.'

So I told him about the show, this huge event, and I told him about how successful the year had been and that we had already met all our commercial targets and that we had a new baby and I was spending a lot of time with our little boy during the day and also spending a lot of time up at night and that I was tired.

I told him that because of all these factors, I didn't really know if I wanted the event to go ahead and that maybe this wasn't the right time, that perhaps I should wait until I was less tired, until our little girl started sleeping.

There were a lot of maybes in my story so eventually I asked him what he thought.

Ravi, in his normal, sensitive, compassionate and kind way, said, 'Gerry, do you want me to answer honestly?'

'Of course,' I said. We have always spoken honestly to each other.

'OK, Gerry,' he said, and in that moment, as I looked down at the floor while lying on the bed, I felt his hand hit me on my back with full force. It was like he had given me a karate chop right into the middle of my back, which instantly shocked me into full attention.

'What was that?' I asked.

'That was a wake-up call,' he said. 'It is time you woke up. You're looking for energy in the wrong place – you're looking to the body for energy when you know the body is tired. For this show to be the show you want it to be, you are going to need an abundance of energy and that energy can't come from the body: the body doesn't have it. But that doesn't mean you can't find it. You must look for the energy not in a place that's of limited energy like the body but a place of infinite energy like the soul.' Then he asked, 'Why did you start your business in the first place, Gerry? Why do you want to do these shows? What was the vision at the beginning?'

I told him about our mission statement: in times of darkness, light the little light you have and welcome the weary traveller.

'Well, what does that mean to you?' Ravi asked me. 'In times of darkness, light the little light you have and welcome the weary traveller – is it in all times or just sometimes? Is it only when you have energy, only when you're not tired, only when it suits you? Is this mission statement defined and dependent on your state of energy, your state of mind, on your emotions? Is it something you do when you feel like it and something you don't do when you don't feel like it? Is this a sometimes mission? Or is this a life statement, a statement about who you are and what you believe, not just sometimes but all times? And who are you getting your mission from?

If your mission is to simply build a business and meet your commercial targets, then once they are met you won't have energy for anything else. But if your mission is coming from something deeper, something bigger, then your mission has to be steadfastly committed to something that gives you energy and drives you with love.

'People are looking to you,' he continued, 'people are tired, people are scared, people are doubting themselves and they are feeling exactly like you feel now, Gerry, and they are looking for hope, they are looking for inspiration, they are looking for a glimmer of light. They are looking for someone to tell them what to do with their fear and their tiredness. Now is the moment, Gerry, you either step up or you step out. You and only you can answer what your mission is, you and only you can answer why you are putting on this show and only you know where this mission is coming from.

'When you close your eyes,' he said, 'can you visualise the people who are coming to the show who are scared or feeling empty and alone and can you see yourself providing a day of music, meditation and talks that inspires them and gives them a sense of hope and light and allows them to discover their own light? Can you imagine how this would feel to be able to do this for those people?'

Something in me began to switch; something started to ignite and awaken.

He continued, 'Can you see those people leaving with a sense of energy and passion? You have the gift of handing people their light back, you have an opportunity to allow people to see their inner light when they have lost their own, you have a chance to be a guiding light, a voice of truth, a voice of inspiration and a reflection of the divine and either now you step into that without condition or you step away from it because the divine mission doesn't do exception and we don't get to pick and choose what pieces we take on – we either take it on fully and unconditionally or we don't. You don't bring the divine on your journey; the divine brings you on its journey.

'I thought you were a Christian,' he said, 'I thought you understood the story of Jesus and the crucifixion. Jesus had to embrace the entire journey, the entire mission, he didn't get to pick the nice bits and avoid the painful bits. He didn't get to choose the journey – the only choice he had was to step into it or not.'

Ravi stopped for a second, as if to check if he had said too much or to see how I was going to react.

But before I responded, he continued, 'Gerry you have been given a gift and you have been given a mission. Think of Noah who built the ark. When the world was drowning, Noah built the ark. But nobody ever asked if Noah was interested in building boats or whether he was tired or stressed or whether he was busy, or whether it suited him or not to build the ark. He accepted his mission, and he built the ark.

'Sometimes different things appear in our life. There are moments when our mission becomes clear and often it is not us that gives us that mission: it is handed to us from somewhere and someone bigger and deeper than ourselves.

'The world is drowning in darkness and fear, Gerry, and you have been asked to build a boat, a boat of honesty, of love and of connection. If this is something you're interested in, if this is something that sets your soul on fire, then step up and build the boat; and if it's not, tell the divine that you're not interested, that you're too tired, it's too hard to sell tickets and you've already met your targets. Tell the divine all your excuses and as you hear yourself saying them see how they feel, not in your head but in your heart and in your soul.'

As Ravi spoke, I could feel something inside me bubble up, an energy, a passion, a fire. Something was awakening inside of me and within minutes the tired body I'd walked in with had disappeared, the tired mind, the tired brain and the excuses had disappeared and all I could see was a show filled to the roof with amazing people. I could feel and sense the music, the meditation, and I could feel the arena filled with raw human spirit.

I knew this was my mission. It wasn't in my brain, but it was in my soul. My soul was screaming at me to put this on, to step up and live my mission with fearlessness, to step firmly into it because it had all the energy I needed. My soul was asking me to trust it and to give myself fully to my mission and somehow it would all make perfect sense and somehow I would find the energy and the passion to deliver something truly special.

I remember jumping off the bed at the end of the session. I was like a new man; I was clear and I was focused.

It became so clear in my mind: no wonder tickets weren't selling. Because my energy towards the show was negative, it was limited and non-committed. I didn't really know if I wanted to hold the show or not, so how would people know whether they should go or not? Ravi said as long as my energy was saying, *I don't know, I'm not sure*, then the people thinking of buying a ticket, the people going to click the link, would get that far and then they would be unsure also. Right now the universe was matching my energy and the stagnation of ticket sales was a reflection of my stagnated energy. Change your energy, change the universe.

I left with a new sense of something powerful inside me, a deep sense that the show had already happened and it was a deeply powerful experience. The doubts had disappeared. I didn't care about ticket sales; the people that needed to be there would be there and the number of people there was irrelevant. What those who attended it would experience was where I was now putting my energy.

On my way home, a really good friend of mine, Trisha Lewis, phoned me out of the blue to say that she was meant to do an Instagram Live with somebody that evening, but they had pulled out at the last moment. She asked if by any chance I would be interested in stepping in. 'Absolutely,' I told her. I jumped on that Instagram Live that night and I spoke about what happened with Ravi; I spoke about my mission and my passion and my vision for the show. I told her I wanted to create a space of inspiration, of light and of life to inspire and motivate. I just spoke freely. I wasn't speaking from my brain anymore; I wasn't speaking from my tired body. I was speaking from my energised soul.

Somehow it radiated, it resonated with the listeners. Shortly after the Instagram session the ticket sales started to fly. People had heard me speak about the show in a new way, in a new energy, in a new frequency. And for the remainder of the week, ticket sales just accelerated. Two weeks later, somehow, miraculously, the show was sold out.

Ravi had awoken something inside me, he had changed my energy, my frequency, and when I started beaming that energy and frequency out into the universe, the universe listened, and the show sold out.

One of the most important questions Ravi asked me while we were having that conversation was what was taking my energy, what was fatiguing me. He asked if I was to know that the show was a sell-out, that it could change the lives of all those who attended, would I have enough energy? Of course, the answer was yes.

'So, what's depleting your energy?' he asked. 'You're too focused on ticket sales, on the logistics, on the how and the what, and you're not focused enough on the why.'

It was a great reminder that when we focus on the why, when we live with truth and passion, even without the presence of a how and a what, somehow, miraculously, the universe improvises, the universe meets us. The universe meets passion with opportunity, and it meets passion with process.

We have to step fully into our mission. We must get beyond our brain, beyond our physical body, and step up and ignite our soul to its most alive, its most passionate, its most joyful expression: we must awaken our unconquerable soul.

Sometimes we don't choose our path, sometimes our path is handed to us and the choice we get is whether we live it or not, whether we accept it and embrace our magnificence or whether we hide from it, pretending and convincing ourself we are not enough and we don't have enough. The universe is incredibly intelligent, it knows our mission and it knows us, so we need to trust it, trust ourself and say yes.

We need to step firmly into the callings of our soul, step with confidence into the mission that we've been handed, whether it is one that we predicted, anticipated or wanted. We need to ask ourself this question: if we knew this mission could liberate and help people, if we knew our mission would make the world a better place, if we knew our mission would set us free, would we do it? Then we should go do it, trust the universe, trust ourself.

We can't be half committed; we can't have half our energy in one thing and half in the other and expect them to thrive. Sometimes the universe is simply asking us to commit fully and the moment we do it meets us with everything we need.

'We must get beyond our brain, beyond our physical body, and step up and ignite our soul to its most alive, its most passionate, its most joyful expression: we must awaken our unconquerable soul.'

Sometimes we have to take the first step, even when we can't see the second step; sometimes we have to answer that calling that is deep in our soul and sometimes we have to trust the universe and we have to step out and trust that a step will appear. And from my experience, every time I have, every time I have listened to my heart and soul and taken the first step, the second step has arrived and the third and so on. Our brain simply cannot see what our soul can see and our brain can never feel what our soul is connected to; our heart always knows the way and our soul will always lead us home. Even if we can't see the how, knowing the why and allowing this to be the powerful force that drives us will always be enough.

Know your why, give everything meaning and live with intent

Very often in life we look to the world to give us meaning. People ask, 'What is the meaning of life? What is the meaning of the universe?' Having thought about these questions for much of my life, having struggled with them, having chased external things for validation and for meaning, I have come to the realisation that meaning is in fact not an outside thing; it is not an objective thing. I believe now more than ever that meaning is a subjective thing. That which gives great meaning and joy to one person might be devoid of meaning and joy for another person.

I think we are all realising as we awaken to a new level of human consciousness that each and every one of us has a responsibility to bring our own meaning to life. We need to ask: 'Who am I? Why am I here? What is the purpose of my life?' When we begin to give something a new meaning, just like in life and sport, then we begin to embrace it in a whole new way. What we do in life doesn't matter as much as why we do it. In fact, when we start to think about why we do something we begin to realise how powerful we can be. Think about a chair that weighs 100 kg and ask people, 'Do you think you can lift that?' Most will quickly scan through their conscious brain and ask themselves, *Do I go to the gym? Do I regularly lift 100 kg?* and they will answer, 'No.' If you reframe the question and say, 'What if your three-year-old daughter is trapped underneath the chair and the only way she will survive is if you lift the chair three inches. Now do you think you could lift it? Of course, the answer is yes. The most important question then is what would that chair have to weigh before you would think about not lifting it? Of course, the answer is, 'If I love that person, it wouldn't matter what the chair weighed, I would do my very best to lift it. I would give it a go.' When we apply that to life, instead of a chair that we need to lift, what about the opportunity that we never took? The dream we never pursued? The job we never applied for? The person we didn't say hello to? How many times in life do we actually talk ourselves out of something and decide we can't do it before we even try? I believe we do that not because we don't know what we want, not because we don't know how to do it. I think at times we fall short and let opportunities slip because we don't apply a *why*. We don't know *why* so in the instance of the chair that weighs 100 kg it's easy to say no until we apply a meaning. If the meaning is saving the life of someone we love, suddenly we activate a new superpower. We move beyond fear and when something is important enough, when our mind, our body and our spirit are all connected to that one thing in that moment, when our *why* ignites, we will always find a way. Viktor Frankl, in his incredible book *Man's Search for Meaning*, has that simple but beautiful line which states that anyone who uncovers their why will discover their how. Whatever your goals, your targets, whatever the mission, the adventure you are setting out on, don't just ask, 'How do I do it?' Also ask, 'Why am I doing it?' Before you write down any goal ask yourself, 'Why is this important?' He who has a why will find a how and he who has not got a why struggles to find the how.

Press Pause

Think about whatever your goals are, whatever the mission, or adventure you are setting out on. Have you been asking yourself 'How do I do this?' Now ask yourself why are you doing it?

Before you write down any goal ask yourself, 'Why is this important?'

He who has a why will find a how and he who has not got a why, struggles to find the how.

---

10. Surrender

Very often in life we are taught that to surrender is a sign of weakness and a negative act. However, I have come to learn that when we reframe how we perceive surrendering it can be one of the most emotionally powerful acts there is. In order to be able to live in an ever-changing world, where at times we have so little control, the ability to surrender is not a weak acceptance but a powerful choice to emotionally let go of our attachments.

Surrendering is an act of immense strength and courage. I believe surrender is an invitation to freedom, growth and transformation. It opens the door to a new chapter in our lives, where we willingly release control and trust in the flow of the universe. Surrendering doesn't mean we're weak; it means we're strong enough to let go of our attachments, fears and expectations. It's about recognising that there are forces greater than ourselves at play and understanding that we can't always control every outcome. Surrender allows us to tap into a higher power and surrender ourselves to the magic of life. When we surrender, we create space for miracles. We let go of resistance and become open to new possibilities and opportunities. Surrender becomes a catalyst for growth.

It was 4 a.m. and the sun was beginning to appear over the Alps. The moon and a single star were still present in the sky overhead and at that moment it was neither morning nor night: it was the very special time where morning meets night, the special time between the past and the future, that special time where the energy seems a little different. Ahead of me I saw a stream of tiny lights making their way up this incredible mountain that dwarfs all else, including us humans who were attempting to summit it. In that moment I was struck by how small the lights on the helmets of the climbers were, how vulnerable we were, how much at the mercy of this incredible mountain we were – an avalanche, a rock fall, a crack in the ice, a slip into a 100-metre crevasse and that was the end. Never had my life been so exposed, so vulnerable and so in the hands of nature.

As I stood there surrounded by so much threat and so much danger, my thinking brain and my ego started to do everything that they are meant to do – to protect me by:
1. Taking me away from the danger
2. Controlling the situation

Deep in my heart I wanted to climb higher to see the sunrise from the summit. My brain was saying run away, but my heart was saying you might never get this opportunity again, and every fibre of my heart was asking me to put one foot in front of the other and just keep moving. But my thinking brain kept trying to control the situation. I was asking the guide a million 'what if?' questions a second, trying to reassure myself that he had everything covered and that we were the ones in control in this situation. At one point he stopped me, and in a quiet and assured way he said: 'Gerry, you are looking for assurance I can't give you and I am not in the business of lying. Climbing high mountains is risky, it's foolish to think it isn't, we have gone through all this and you signed up. I can pretend we can control the mountain if you like, but we can't. We have taken every precaution we can but even then we must accept the risk and we have to bow to the mountain and its incredible power. No human is ever going to be more powerful than this mountain, and the moment you think you are, you shouldn't be here. Mountain-climbing comes with certain rules and acceptances and accepting that it is risky and the mountain is more powerful is the only way you can be at peace here. It's about humility, not strength or control; the more we try to control the mountain, the more we lose sight of what we are here to do.'

And that's when I realised. We can talk about conquering the mountain but we can never conquer it. The mountain exists whether we climb it or not and will continue to exist long after we have left it. But maybe we can conquer something inside ourselves: our fears, our need to be in control, our self-doubt. And we see that the summit we are trying to reach is actually inside of us: our dreams, our identity, our souls.

On the side of that mountain, in the semi-dark of the dawn, with the sun rising over the Alps, I was having one of the greatest lessons of my life: life is a risk. We can't control it. We don't know why we are born or why we die. We are never more powerful than the universe and the moment we meet this truth with vulnerability and acceptance is the moment we no longer struggle with life. The mountain guide was not giving me any false certainties. He was honest about the rules of climbing and maybe we have to be honest with ourselves about the rules of life: falling in love is risky, daring to pursue our dreams is risky, having children is risky and, no matter what we acquire in life or the people we find to love, at one point we will have to leave them all behind. We can try to shy away from these truths, to suppress them, deny them or control them – but, in fact, we can't.

Maybe life, like the mountain, is something we must bow to, be in awe of, witness without judgement and embrace without fear. And the final pillar to emotional freedom is simply a powerful surrendering to all the things we don't know and can't control. True emotional freedom is accepting that life is risk and that nothing lasts forever, the only thing that matters is what you do with the time you have. You can spend your life trying to predict, control, resist, chasing the next thing, or you can simply surrender to the great unknown, the great and incredible mystery that is this universe and is this thing we call life.

Whether we like to accept it, talk about it or not, us humans are always at the mercy of this vast universe and, despite the illusions of the power we think we have, we have little power over the big things, like the sun rising, the earth's rotation, the fields of gravity and the millions of permutations that have to happen in order for us to simply exist. At any moment the universe can change our plans, our future and our destiny. Power to control is an illusion. The real power comes from the freedom to be vulnerable, to be at the mercy of the unfolding, uncontrollable phenomenon we call the universe and, in that place of vulnerability, be at peace. True emotional health exists in the freedom to be at peace within the unknown.

We must listen to the callings of our heart and not be afraid of the vastness and uncertainty of the universe but meet it with a sense of awe and see it as something we belong to and not as something to fear.

As I looked at the tiny lights that stretched out across the side of the mountain ahead of me, slowly but surely making their way up, it reminded me of the incredible bravery and enormous ambition that is at the heart of human beings. It reminded me that, as small as we may be, we are not insignificant and when our hearts are awoken and filled with passion and love we can scale even the greatest mountains and challenges. We somehow have the ability to engage with the power and awesomeness of the universe and not be intimidated by it, not retreat from it. As we walked along through the snow, still in semi-darkness, I noticed the beautiful silence. Each climber was making their way up, connected to one another by a rope but at least 10 metres apart, which made communication almost impossible. So each climber spent hours alone with their own thoughts and alone with their own mission.

Each of us had come there for a reason, either to find something or to leave something behind, and in the silence of the morning we had an amazing opportunity to find the answer to our questions and hear it for ourselves. Far too often in life we experience unnecessary noise, unnecessary conversations. The presence of all this noise makes it almost impossible to go inward and hear our deepest inner voice and the whisper of our own soul. Here in the beautiful and peaceful silence we had no choice but to be at one with our own thoughts and we had no choice but to hear what our hearts and souls were actually asking us for. Emotional health is about getting out of the noise of the thinking brain and getting into the silent whispers of our heart and our soul.

'Emotional health is about getting out of the noise of the thinking brain and getting into the silent whispers of our heart and our soul.'

There in that moment, surrounded by the vastness of the mountain, I was never more vulnerable. I never had less control of my own life yet I never felt so at ease, so at peace, so connected and so at one with everything. It was like in the vastness of the mountain I was disappearing, and as I let go of my need to control, to predict, to understand, as I let go of all the things that I think make me and all the things I think make me different, it was like the temporary Gerry was disappearing into the mountain so that I was no longer separate from the mountain. I was no longer climbing the mountain or trying to conquer it, I was simply part of the mountain, part of its story, and the mountain was part of the sky, and in that moment I experienced an extraordinary, powerful sense of connection to all things, at that moment I was at one with everything. My ego had bowed to the magnificent mystery and power of the universe, and by releasing myself from all limits and labels, it was like I had disappeared from the physical Gerry and had become awareness, where I could experience the energy field that connects all things and I could experience the frequency of awe.

Maybe the ultimate state of emotional health and freedom is simply living with a powerful sense of awe when we realise that we are the connected energy field and that we are the universe looking at itself and witnessing its own magnificence. Maybe true freedom appears when we realise that the universe is not a mystery to be solved or an enemy to be defended against but simply a mystery to be witnessed and to be in awe of. Maybe emotional freedom isn't a place or state of mind, it doesn't require certainty, or predictability, or assurance of the future; maybe it's a feeling, maybe it's a frequency and maybe in our understanding of frequency we discover our true identity and our true existence.

Press Pause

My wife, Miriam Hussey, wrote a beautiful and powerful poem on the theme of the power of surrendering. It is a stunning piece and helps me at crucial times to remember that the gateway to emotional freedom lies in the willingness and ability to surrender.

TO SURRENDER

I believe surrendering is not a deep collapsing, a quitting
    or an inability to cope.
I believe it to be something different.
To surrender is to humbly bow to our vulnerabilities.
It is the softening into our strength.
It is the dissolving away of our anger, judgement, shame
    or blame,
And the melting away of external barriers, the dissolution
    of the walls of protection that we often uphold or
    barricade around us to keep our demons locked in
    and love shielded out.

I believe surrendering is the letting go of resistance and
the grip of control or the need to own. It is the delicate
landing and arriving into who we are and the acceptance
of where we are in this moment.

Surrendering is the space that allows all the home truths
to be seen, heard and felt.

To surrender is to wave the white flag to the peace that
resides within.

Surrendering is to come home to our authentic selves.

To surrender is to come home.

MEDITATION ON SURRENDERING

1. Find a comfortable, quiet space where you can sit or lie
   down in a relaxed position.
2. Close your eyes and take a few deep breaths, allowing
   yourself to settle into the present moment.
3. Bring your attention to the sensation of your breath as
   it enters and leaves your body. Feel the gentle rise and
   fall of your abdomen or the air flowing in and out of your
   nostrils.
4. With each breath, imagine exhaling any tension or
   thoughts that may be weighing you down, letting go of
   control and resistance.
5. As you continue to breathe, repeat a simple mantra
   silently in your mind, such as 'I surrender' or 'I let go'.

Allow these words to become an anchor, reminding you to release any need for outcomes or for clinging to specific outcomes.

6. As you repeat your chosen mantra, notice any sensations or emotions that arise within you. Observe them without judgement, acknowledging their presence without attaching to or trying to change them.

7. Visualise yourself surrendering to the flow of life, like a leaf floating effortlessly on a gentle stream. Imagine the water carrying you forward, trusting in its ability to guide you.

8. As you surrender, feel a sense of relief and lightness, as if a weight has been lifted off your shoulders. Allow yourself to fully embrace this feeling of letting go.

9. Take a few more deep breaths, gradually bringing your attention back to the present moment.

10. When you are ready, gently open your eyes and carry the sense of surrender with you throughout your day.

SUMMARY

- Living with emotional freedom – learning your why
- Separating the work from the tasks
- Our challenges don't get smaller but we can get stronger
- The pillars of emotional freedom
  1. Non-resistance
  2. Non-judgement
  3. Non-attachment
  4. Non-striving
  5. Forgiveness
  6. Non-comparison
  7. Trust
  8. Gratitude
  9. The emotional power of why
  10. Surrender

Conclusion

It's March 2023, and I'm sitting on the beach watching my little boy dig holes in the sand. Beyond him the water washes against the shore in an ever-changing, constant movement that reminds me of the ebb and flow of my life. On the horizon the sun is disappearing – it appears to be going down, but we now know the sun doesn't set or rise; the sun is the ever-present life-giving source of energy that sustains all of life. It is we on the earth that move, not the sun, and as we move into the darkness of the evening, I am reminded that the universe, just like my life, is always moving from dark to light, and just as the sun never sets, the light is always waiting for us to move towards it. It assures me even in my dark moments, when I have emotionally lost my way, that nothing lasts, everything is impermanent and that temporary feeling will subside and give way to a brighter one as long as

I am willing to do the work to create the change. I am more comfortable than ever with the impermanence of everything, my thoughts, my emotions, my life situations and even life itself. The less I see myself as a disconnected entity and the more I see myself as simply a temporary manifestation of the infinite field gives me the ability to take every moment as it is and, without judgement, allow it to be what it needs to be before releasing it back into the universe. Nothing lasts for ever and the less we attached our energy, attention and awareness to the temporary situation, the more we see all situations as simply moments in an unfolding dance that we are here to simply observe.

As I look at Eli, my little boy, his silhouette is surrounded by the magnificence of the sun and it's like there is no separation between him and the sun, no separation between him and the beach, it's like it is all one, like he is the sun dancing with itself. As I sit there and watch this connection with this incredible universe, I am reminded that separation only exists in our minds, in our frightened egos, and that once we move beyond the illusion of separation there is a powerful and heart-opening sense of deep connection and deep peace where everything is actually connected.

At that moment, sitting on the sand, I feel connected: to the sun, the moon, the ocean, the sand and above all to my little boy as he sits and is now watching me as if he has just realised that we are all connected and that he is me looking back at myself.

There in that moment is connection, is peace, and in that moment everything makes perfect sense. Life is not about striving or forcing, it's not about light or darkness, it's not about winning or losing, it's not about getting somewhere; in that moment I realise life is about awareness and connection. Awareness that we are connected and that we are the universe looking back at itself. Peace is not about getting to a place where everything is sorted, or controllable or predictable; peace is simply being at ease with what is in that moment without fear, resistance or judgement. Peace has little to do with the outside world and everything to do with our inside choices.

In the morning we return to Ireland; there will be big changes in our lives and in our business, some predictable and lots not, yet in my heart there is peace. I have come to both accept and relish the ever-changing nature of life.

Just as the world is an ever-changing, dynamic process where nothing stays the same, I have accepted that my life will mirror that. I don't need things to stay the same, I no longer need to predict or control, I no longer need to know what the future holds; I simply need to know what my heart is asking me for. Our hearts are always connected to our deepest truths and our hearts always know the answers; our souls are our deepest wisdom, and our souls will always lead us home.

Emotions come and go. They are essential messages that give us incredibly insightful information if we are willing to get to know them, understand them and always remember we are in charge of them, they are not in charge of us. Our emotions are here to serve us; we are not here to serve our emotions.

Our emotions can always be changed and regulated by doing the work outlined in this book. The only negative emotion is the denied or suppressed emotion. Emotions are like clouds: allow them to come but don't attach to them; allow them to go as easily as they appear once you have received the information they want you to have.

To bring me to a place of emotional ease I have examined and reshaped my deepest beliefs and realised that very often it is our inner beliefs that drive our emotions and not the outside world. Maybe the only two questions we really need to answer are:

1. What do you really believe about yourself?
2. What do you really believe about the universe?

I stand up to shake the sand off before I leave. It's time to leave it behind, like shaking off the past, and out of my nervous system and out of my energy field there comes a time where we no longer need to hold the past and there is a time we are free to leave it behind. I feel the warmth of the last of the sun hit my skin and it reminds me of my own energy field, my own source of power and the source from which every other part of me is responding. Taking time every single day to renew and refresh my energy field and shake out of it all that no longer serves me is vital to a life of energy, freshness and renewal.

'Are we going home, Daddy?' my little boy asks.

'Yes,' I reply, but as I stand there in that moment I know I am already home and that home for me is no longer a physical place or geographical location but an inner place of peace, a sense of connection and deep awareness that we are so much more than chemicals and biology, we are so much more than the things that happen to us, we are so much more than our past: we are infinite energy fields with an infinite potential for freedom and love and of all the emotions we can experience love is the most powerful and most freeing.

I hope this book is a reminder for you that you are so much more than your thoughts, your emotions, and that you are so much more than the things that have happened to you and the things that are happening around you. I hope it has helped you to understand emotions in a new way and the power they have to heal or to hurt our body, our mind and our life. I hope this book reminded you that nobody else can generate or maintain an emotion in you only you. Once we begin to resolve the ego and awaken our higher, observer self, we realise that we are not the experience; we are the person experiencing the emotion. We are the peaceful observer that is above all of that, and at all times as the peaceful observer we have the ability to witness and experience our emotions but not be defined by or entangled in them.

I hope this book and the life lessons I have shared will awaken you to a new awareness about the greatest freedom there is – emotional freedom – and that the most important promise we will make is the promise to honour our freedom contract.

Acknowledgements

To my mum, thank you for always being a loving, fun and selfless force that has given me the wings to fly and a fearless courage to explore the world both inside and outside of me. I love you with all my heart.

To my dad, you are my hero. You are a tower of strength and a selfless service. You have been by my side at every step of this journey: the late-night car drives; the cold, empty dressing rooms; the early flights; the packed arenas. Getting to do this is a gift, but getting to do it with my dad by my side is a treasure. I love you more than I can ever express.

To Ciara Doorley, words cannot say how thankful I am for your kindness, your relentless commitment to this book and your belief in me. Every now and again I get the gift of meeting some very special people and you are one of the most special. Thank you for everything.

Faith O'Grady, thank you for not walking away. Thank you for standing with me when it appeared this book might never come. You are an incredible energy of fun and confidence that allows people to believe in themselves. It is an honour to work with you.

To Joanna, Elaine, Bernard, Breda and the entire Hachette team, thank you for staying the course with me and for the amazing journey we have taken since you backed me with writing *Awaken Your Power Within*. I will forever be indebted to you. And thanks for Aonghus Meaney for his edit.

Finally, thank you to the little boy inside of me who never gave up on the idea that he had an important message that needed to be told. Thank you for your vulnerability, your courage, your relentless willingness to fail and your beautiful heart that simply wants to give.

NOTES

NOTES

NOTES

NOTES

NOTES